BARNABAS and PAUL:
Brothers in Conflict

BARNABAS and PAUL:

Brothers in Conflict

John Warren Steen

BROADMAN PRESS
Nashville, Tennessee

ISBN: 0–8054–8703–4

4287–03

Library of Congress Catalog Card Number: 73–80777

Dewey Decimal Classification: F

Printed in the United States of America

To
my mother-in-love
Nell Roeder Lipham

One

THE REDHEADED WOMAN bit Barnabas. He felt pain but refused to yell. Years of training in the wrestling ring had taught him to accept pain. But in the supervised rules of that sport, he had never experienced teeth tearing into his arm.

With his uninjured arm, Barnabas tried to separate the fighting women. The plump one began to pull his curly black hair. He whispered, "Stop, Lydia." The struggle took place not more than twenty paces from the carved cedar doorway of the basilica of law, where a clean-shaven Jewish youth entered, oblivious of their controversy.

Lydia released the teacher's hair and tugged at the red-head's robe with both hands until it ripped. Barnabas put his head between their snorting noses and said, "Stop, sisters." The last word softened the grip of the biter, and Rhoda smoothed down her red hair. The hair-puller put her hands on her hips defiantly. They were sisters—not in the same earthly family, but they were children of God.

Thorn Bush, his sandy hair ablaze in the dusk, raced up to the dispute and shouted: "Women, stop this disgrace. Think of the church." He was not even a member.

Barnabas stood between the women and the basilica. It was the largest meeting place in the city of Antioch, available each evening for the devotees of the new religion. The two women panted and glared at each other as an officer from the Roman Legion helped an aged Syrian to shuffle through the great doors. Barnabas recognized the men and recalled that despite their ages both were catechumens—learners. Those beginners need instructions; they didn't need disillusionment. Barnabas hoped they hadn't heard the commotion, made louder by Thorn Bush's bellowing.

Barnabas said to Thorn Bush: "Don't condemn them. They need your help and also that of the others in the church. They are babes in Christ."

The fat woman, smelling of crushed rose petals and sweat, said, "Barnabas, you're a weakling."

He looked at Thorn Bush. "I almost agree with Lydia. It's been years since I've pulled wrestlers apart. And I've never before tried to separate two mad dogs." He smiled.

Lydia, not smiling, folded her arms, "You're a very strange . . ."

The red-haired slave said, "Don't you call our teacher strange, or I'll spring on you again until . . ."

"Sisters." Again Barnabas used the soothing word, and the women relaxed.

Rhoda said, "You taught us that God forgives. Well, I fought with Lydia, and God will forgive, won't he?" Barnabas nodded assent. "If I fight her again later tonight, he'll still forgive. It's his business to forgive . . ."

"No, you've misunderstood what I tried to teach."

"That's what I tried to tell the couple who are living in adultery," said Thorn Bush, "but they say Barnabas teaches that God forgives every sin."

The Son of Encouragement dropped to his knees. The

close-fitting stones of Tiberius Street felt warm to his knees. A familiar feeling. He recalled stumbling in the streets of his native Cyprus as a drunken youth.

"Let's get back to us," said the slave with flaming hair. "Lydia called you strange."

"I didn't mean it. I love Barnabas." Her chubby hand patted the black waves on his head. He stood.

"Everybody loves the Cypriot," said the younger woman, "but you'd like to have him for your own. Confess."

"That's enough chatter," said Barnabas. He could be firm.

The slave girl looked down at her sandaled toes beneath the torn gown. "I wish you would tell us again what to believe about forgiveness. Barnabas, it seems different every time you explain it. I tried to talk with my mistress—she's very intelligent—but she laughed at me. Called me a fanatic."

Barnabas asked the women to check on the baskets of bread at the front of the basilica. After they left, he put his arm on Thorn Bush's broad shoulder. "Trouble's growing. I've always wanted success. Now, I'm plagued with it. When I left Jerusalem, I hoped to get fifteen or twenty new believers to sign up for the catechumen's class. I never expected . . ."

"Barnabas, I told you before. I tell you again. Go back up to Jerusalem for helpers. You can't do this work alone. There are two hundred and seventy-five people waiting in the basilica to learn from you. They have different needs. But they must be divided into different groups and taught on their own levels."

"You're right about helpers, but Jerusalem can't pull me out of this deep water." He recalled the reason he had left the Holy City. He hadn't volunteered for this job.

Barnabas recalled a cool winter afternoon in Jerusalem about an hour before services were scheduled, when he went to suggest an idea to his aunt and cousin. He found them in the courtyard of their handsome home. No breeze hit them there. They sat on a stone bench and invited him to sit on one of the other three that formed a rectangle. No one mentioned the persecutions. Barnabas was excited over the news he had just heard from a freed slave from Caesarea. "Some of our number have gone to Cyprus. You know that, of course. Now some of the Cypriots have become followers of the Way."

A surprised expression came over the raisin-like face of his mother's sister. "Do you hear that, Mark?" She pulled her son closer to her and hugged the young man who was in his early twenties—Barnabas couldn't remember the exact year. "The Lord's work goes on."

Barnabas said to the woman, "Cyprus would be a good place for you. Safer than Jerusalem. You could live with my mother and explain the Way to her."

John Mark said, "Mother couldn't . . ." His eyes were those of a frightened animal.

"No, Barnabas, I want to keep the upper room open for services as long as there is a believer left in Jerusalem." Many believers had been looking for reasons to leave the dangerous city, but not his aunt. She squeezed his hand, "You go to Cyprus."

He visualized the dye vats of his mother's home, his synagogue, and a little boy who had pleaded years ago to come along with him on the trip to Jerusalem. He wondered if it would look like cowardice for him to book passage back to the beautiful island. "I would like . . ."

"No, not yet!" The voice was Simon Peter's. No one had seen him enter the arbor-filtered twilight of the courtyard. "No." He jolted them with a return to his brusque manner of previous years. His full brown beard melted into his robe of the same shade. "I have received a message from Caesarea that believers from Cyprus have taken the message to Antioch."

"We just heard from a freed slave that . . ."

"I also heard," said Peter, "from the man who freed him, Cornelius. He has learned that some of the Cypriots and believers from Cyrene went to Antioch and gave the message to Gentiles there."

Barnabas saw the evening star.

Mark looked puzzled. "Gentiles accepting the Messiah?"

The fisherman paced back and forth as he talked. "Someone must go to Antioch to investigate. James believes that Gentiles are being accepted into the church without circumcision or any instruction in the law." Peter walked over to the bench and put his hand on Barnabas' shoulder. "You can do it."

Barnabas stood. He was almost as tall as Peter. "Let James go for himself."

"He wants to. That's the trouble. He's going to ask the church tonight. Barnabas, think what could happen. You know how unbending he is about the most trivial law; he's always right—anybody who disagrees is wrong. On a matter as important as circumcision, he would . . . Don't you see how he could offend new believers, babes in Christ? You should take a committee and make this investigation for us."

Barnabas pulled a grape from the arbor and rubbed it clean on his sleeve. "I'll go on my own terms, and I think they're within the Lord's will."

"What are they?"

"I must go alone. I'd raise fewer questions that way. And I won't accept any time schedule for reporting back to the church here." Peter agreed. The aunt hugged Barnabas, and he caught a whiff of onions on her breath. "Mark, will you make me a copy of the crucifixion story?"

"Well, I can see the need for converts to have it, but— Mother, do you think I can finish it?"

She nodded.

"I'll start after the service. But I must add the resurrection story."

The apostle said: "We'll discuss this journey tonight at the service and vote on your going as our representative. The trip could be the most important of your life if . . ."

"If what?"

"If the Lord doesn't return and bring in his kingdom first." No one looked at the other. They moved like a flock of sheep to another pasture, climbing the wooden steps to the upper room.

Simon Peter was persuasive at the meeting. He had to be to convince someone as stubborn as James that Barnabas should be the one to make a trip to investigate. After the final dedicatory prayer, Lydia, Rhoda, and other brothers and sisters in the faith hugged the Son of Encouragement and wished him God's blessings. A certain woman said nothing, but he saw her blue robe disappear through the door and down the steps. He knew he could see her later.

James said in private that he was gravely concerned about the situation and didn't want anybody to get the idea that the Law was unimportant. Peter expressed concern about

Barnabas' safety and particularly warned him about robbers from Tyre northward.

Nicolaus, the proselyte from Antioch who had long ago turned to Judaism and then recently to the Jesus religion, now one of the Seven, warned Barnabas of the natives. "They're pagan to the core. Steal the sandals off your feet without your ever knowing. Fun-loving people, though —you'll enjoy them. Just keep your eyes open."

Barnabas returned to his quarters in the home of Zadok the potter. Knowing that he would leave before the doves began their dawn cooing, he went in to say good-by to the withered old man. Zadok was too weak to get out of bed. The girl in the blue robe, Sarah, moistened his lips with goat butter, just as she had for Barnabas when nursing him back to health. The Cypriot saw tears trapped in her long black eyelashes, and he knew that she hadn't wanted to say farewell at the meeting or now. Jacob, almost through with his apprenticeship in pottery, was too big a boy to cry. He looked uncomfortable, shifting his weight. He was eating a pomegranate, spitting out a seed into his left hand every few minutes.

Before dawn Barnabas went out past the kiln and took his donkey, Olivia, from her stall. As they reached the Fish Gate, the sky had turned a rosy color, and the cursing gatekeeper opened the creaky doors of the massive portal. Waiting there was John Mark, with wide eyes and sparse beard, pacing back and forth, looking like a ship without a rudder. Mark hugged his cousin and put around his neck a leather thong to which was attached a rolled-up parchment, the story of the crucifixion and resurrection.

Barnabas and Olivia left by the highway heading west by

northwest. A chariot on its way to Caesarea passed them. After several hours of silence except for the clopping of her hoofs, he said, "Olivia, remember our first trip over this road?" He recalled his attraction for and dread of the Holy City. Now, with a similar mixture of feelings, he headed for Antioch of Syria.

At the port of Caesarea, he stopped by the arched porticos of the harbor warehouses to ask about passage to Cyprus. A captain with a wart on his nose made him a good price on a ship that would weigh anchor within twenty-four hours. The Son of Consolation knew he couldn't disappoint his brothers and sisters who had entrusted him with a duty. He would have chosen rowing on the bottom tier of a galley to this task of judge and prosecutor.

To get his mind off this terrible concern, he decided he would visit the only Cypriot he knew in that great capital city. He headed for the beautiful House of the Laughing Satyr. Cornelia did not meet the door, of course, but the white-haired slave who did recognized him and asked him inside. While waiting to see the wealthy woman who had given him Olivia, he looked back to the atrium. There he saw the boy satyr jumping with his dog—boisterous marble creatures, unmoved by the death angel that knew its way to this house of mosaic floors and exotic foods. The slave came back and said his mistress refused to see a religious fanatic.

Disappointed, Barnabas left by the coastal route, traveled parallel to the aqueduct for almost three hours. He saw the Carmel range and wished for an assurance like fiery Elijah's. Next day he passed the beach where natives said glass was first discovered. Then he came into the country that Jezebel had polluted with temples of Baal and filthy priests who differed little from pimps. One day he passed a place where divers were bringing up murex shells and handing them to women to process for extracting purple dye, and he thought of the bubbling cauldrons of his mother.

The nights of the trip he spent under the stars, sleeping next to Olivia to keep warm. As he neared the River Adonis, he heard some veiled women mourning the god of vegetation who had died during the hot, dry days of summer. He tried to preach to them, but they wouldn't interrupt their superstitious ritual. The nearer to Antioch the milestones showed him to be, the more concerned he grew over the terrible task of reporting on the orthodoxy of the church members. He tried to recall the last time he had quarreled with another who disagreed with his own views. Even in Jerusalem, he had never spoken harshly to Peter about his own shock over the deaths of Ananias and Sapphira. He hadn't agreed with Peter's views on God's wrath. But he still loved the old fisherman.

On the afternoon of the twentieth day, the traveler came in sight of Mount Silpius. Barnabas told the slow-trodding Olivia she wouldn't have to travel much longer. His haste to get into the city before nightfall was impeded by a dozen male celebrants heading for the groves of a beautiful garden park. They entered a stone archway that bore the inscription, *Daphne.* Across the road from the entrance, a young man beside a broken cart beckoned to him from a ditch. Barnabas wanted to ignore the wave, but he felt he must see what the fellow wanted.

The stranger had sand-colored bushy hair. "My name's Thorn Bush." Barnabas looked quizzical. "Everybody in Antioch has a nickname. What's yours and what work are you . . ."

Barnabas heard a noise behind him and whirled around to see five young desert-tanned men sauntering toward him. They came out of the Daphne entrance. He knew he was trapped. In other times, he had protected little Jacob from bullies or a church sister from wild-eyed persecutors. Now, the matter was different. If he tried to fight the six men, he might get injured so badly the believers in Antioch would be burdened with his upkeep for weeks. If he died, the church of Antioch would be blamed by Jerusalem. The former wrestler knew he mustn't fight or he would hurt the church. Surrender was a new experience for him, as sour as a green grape.

When the robbers loosened the money bag from his waist, Barnabas smelled wine on their breaths. He noticed women's makeup rubbed off on the cheek of one and the neck of another. They took nothing else except his leather neckpiece and parchment. "Here's a good luck amulet," sang one who had a long nose and protruding teeth.

"I need that. Don't take . . ." They laughed and pushed him into the ditch with Thorn Bush. Barnabas expected the bushy-haired stranger to go with them. "You're their decoy, aren't you?"

"Never seen them before." His hands were a dark color. "But if I do—when I do—I won't let them forget what they did." Thorn Bush kicked his cart and scattered leather bundles around the dried grass of the ditch. One landed against the Roman roadmarker that designated five miles into town.

"They didn't harm me." Barnabas patted the donkey. "And Olivia's all right. Wonder why they didn't steal her?"

As the two men lifted the cart, Thorn Bush explained a

local superstition about owning an ass. They slid the wheel back on the axle. The weathered wood of the spokes was waxed and polished as neatly as any Roman chariot. They talked about Daphne as they reloaded bundles of tanned goat hides, pungent and clean smelling. "This place sets our city apart from other Antiochs, you know?" Thorn Bush grabbed the handles of the pushcart and started toward the metropolis. "There are four other Antiochs nearby, not counting Antioch in Pisidia. There's only one Antioch-by-Daphne."

"Everybody knows," said Barnabas, "that Antioch is the third largest city in the Empire. Why does it need anything else to distinguish it?" He was glad the new friend was moving at a brisk pace.

"It doesn't really. But the fun-loving people of this place are proud of the reputation of this grove you've just passed. I've never been there, but I've heard of its gushing fountains and tall cypresses. The place is sacred to Daphne and her twin, Apollo. There young men chase the girls they desire." He grinned.

"Must be quite a temptation for all the young men around here."

"Awesome. I think I'll go sometime to investigate what happens. The commander of the Roman Legion has placed it off limits for his troops."

He had used the word *investigate,* and Barnabas thought of James. He imagined the kind of lecture the Lord's brother would give this stranger if he were here, bringing out legal strictures and penalties, likely alluding to stoning and probably ending up with the fire and brimstone of Sodom. The Son of Encouragement chose to change the subject. "Do you know a tanner from Joppa called Simon?"

"Never met him. But I've seen some of his work. You should feel how soft the leather is that he tans. Almost like silk from Damascus. Wish I had a load of it now. I don't care to meet the man. They say he's trying to be a little Christ, whatever that means."

"He'd be honored to have that said about him. I've met him. You'd like him. He's never been a very welcome person at the synagogue. You know what I mean?"

"I ought to. I've been a leather merchant since I was fifteen. I don't do the actual tanning—most of the time—but I handle the finished product. Means a lot of travel. Still, strict Jews keep me at a distance."

"Are there many Jews in Antioch?" It was a selfish question—he knew after he'd asked it. Barnabas wanted to find out what to expect for himself. He should have talked about his new friend's problems.

"Jews have been here since the founding of the city some 350 years ago. More come in all the time, lured by prosperity." The replaced wheel clinked but continued to turn on the heavily traveled road. Barnabas could hear echoes of another clink—golden coins that had dropped into his palms in the past. "Hebrews were in the founder's army. The veterans were given land around the town as a reward for their services. Many began as orchard tenders or farmers or shepherds. In recent years, most have left the fields for the town shops."

"Are they strict in their religion?"

"On any road, most people travel down the middle. A few will take a different course, far to one side or the other. The Jews are like that here. Most are just middle-of-the-road people. They speak Greek along with others. They have civic pride. Of course, they refuse to intermarry, and they insist on circumcision for every baby boy and every proselyte."

The golden moment had dawned for Barnabas to ask the sandy-haired stranger. But the man veered toward a cross-road. "Here's the road I take to the tannery." He pushed his cart toward the secondary road that paralleled the walls.

Barnabas knew he must ask it then or perhaps never: "Have you heard about Jesus the Nazarene?"

"No. Maybe I'll meet him someday." He laughed and waved farewell.

At the city gate, a salesman who offered silver and bronze Daphne trinkets to tourists was gathering up his display. Slanting rays of the setting sun turned the silver items a rosy color and made the bas-relief stand out on the gate behind the vendor. Barnabas glanced above the gates that were twice as big as Jerusalem's and saw carved figures with a man's head, a lion's body, and an eagle's wings. As Barnabas passed through the gate, he recalled the descriptions of the cherubim that had stood sentinel over the tree of life in Eden.

The weary traveler from Jerusalem suspiciously entered a magnificent avenue. He was not too exhausted to notice that the way was paved with close-fitting white stones and colonnaded with Corinthian columns. He found the thoroughfare led straight to a plaza where the other main street intersected with it, a focal point with a gigantic column topped by a sculpture of the former Emperor Tiberius, now dead these seven years. The Cypriot wouldn't have been surprised if the memorial had been to the goddess of love.

A seller of dried figs asked, "How do you like our city?" Barnabas realized that the way he and Olivia had ambled to that busy crossroads where everyone else was hurrying indicated they were strangers. "It's like another Rome, isn't it? But Antioch has its beautiful, swift-running Orontes, more pleasing than the Tiber, don't you think?"

The tired stranger reported that he had never been to Rome. He asked the man directions for finding the Jewish section.

"Just at the base of the rising mountain, not too far from the Cherubim Gate. You passed within a short distance of it when you first entered," the fruit seller said.

Barnabas thanked the man and told him he was sorry he had no money. "Then you'll have a hard time in this city," he smiled, showing some spaces where teeth had rotted out or been broken out.

The stranger passed a shrine to the Maccabean martyrs and knew he had reached the Jewish section. His mood was not what he had planned. Barnabas had been robbed of his money and his parchment. He was exhausted.

He located a clean inn that served food, had an inside latrine, and nurtured a small vineyard in the courtyard. He took a room on the ground floor, with a promise of payment, giving his donkey over as collateral.

One of the men gathered in the refectory yelled out, "Guess we'll have to pay taxes to the Romans until Messiah comes." Barnabas opened his mouth to give the grumbling men the information they needed, but he hesitated. If he told them his beliefs and if they were as intolerant as some of the elders in Jerusalem, he might disappear in the night, never to be heard of by the Antioch believers. I'll find the Followers of the Way, and I'll find my crucifixion parchment tomorrow, he thought as he headed for bed.

For him Antioch was like a promised land that he must

spy out before moving in for a conquest. During his first morning, Barnabas discovered that the synagogues were centers of instruction. Inquirers from other religions were numerous and seemed magnetically drawn from the confused mass of polytheistic legends and immoral practices to the simplicity and purity of monotheism. Synagogue teaching majored on the essentials of the faith, leaving fine points of theology for the scribes in Jerusalem to argue about.

Other guests at the inn and local craftsmen told him about the people who went in for the latest fad of mystery religions. Some citizens worshiped the gods of Egypt, as did a jolly cheesemaker who invited Barnabas to his home for the midday meal, a conversation about Isis, and a short nap before returning to work. Barnabas refused the hospitality and headed for the Tiberius crossroad. Other people were going home, but the visitor headed for the base of the column in the center of the city. As he neared the monument, he saw a fluff of hair like sand-colored wool. Thorn Bush waved to him. "I've been waiting for you."

"I wondered if I'd ever see you again." Barnabas hit him good naturedly on the shoulder.

"The whole world passes by this crossroads. Wait long enough and you'll see everybody." Thorn Bush untied the rope at the Cypriot's waist and to the amazement of his friend placed on it the familiar leather moneybag.

"Where . . . ? How . . . ?"

"One of the robbers—the bucktoothed one—took the money from the others at a tavern last night. As he was trying to escape at dawn, I saw him just outside the city gate. I'd recognize him anywhere. I chased him until he dropped the money. Is it all there?"

Barnabas ran his fingertips over the smooth leather pouch and then let the rays of the midday sun fall inside the bag. "Most of it's here. But how about the parchment?"

"Probably gave it to some woman," Thorn Bush said. "But don't worry about something so trivial. You've got your money back!" The merchant said he had to deliver some orders of sheepskin. He asked the location of the inn where Barnabas was staying, and they walked back that far together. Thorn Bush said he'd still like to catch the buck-toothed bandit, and he left to make his deliveries.

Barnabas had studied each woman that passed him. None wore the leather necklace. As he prayed for God to lead him to it, he saw a red-haired girl stumble in the street in front of his inn. Bearded men at the food and drink counter that opened on the street ignored her except for a youth who laughed at her.

As Barnabas helped the young woman to her feet, his eyes focused on her leather thong necklace. "Does that hold a rolled-up parchment?"

She wiped some wine from her chin. "How did you know? Did you sell it to Hawk?"

"No, someone stole it from me. Can I buy it back?"

"Here. If it's stolen, I'm afraid to keep it—might have a curse." As she lifted the necklace over her head, it caught a long strand of copper-colored hair. "Hawk will probably kill me. But he won't see me where I'm going tonight."

Barnabas was concerned for her safety. "Do you plan to see another man?"

"Oh, no, I'm going to meet with some strange people who worship Christ and find out if they are really cannibals."

The confused words from the curious young woman were

a trumpet blast for Barnabas. His day of spying out the land was over. It was time for the campaign to begin.

The meeting place was a bake shop on Jawbone Street near the pantheon. The aroma of recently baked bread lingered about the place as he stood before the group. A plump woman stood and screamed: "This is the man I told you about. In Jerusalem, I saw him give gold coins to the church."

As he waited for the chattering to stop, Barnabas noticed a sand-colored bushy head at the door and waved to Thorn Bush. The Son of Encouragement unrolled the parchment with its red hair still attached and began to read about the events that happened on Golgotha. Just as he read the words, "My God, my God, why has thou forsaken me?" he saw a beautiful head of copper hair gleaming in the lamplight. When the young woman looked up, her face was so bruised that both eyes were almost swollen shut. At the conclusion of the reading, there was a deep silence. The baker host came up and whispered a request for a second reading. Barnabas read, and the people listened. He noticed that Thorn Bush wiped a tear from his cheek, and the red-headed girl sobbed aloud.

A Roman soldier said to the group: "I would like to bring ten friends with me tomorrow night, but where could we put them? Even tonight, people are standing out in Jawbone Street."

Barnabas told the people about the basilica of law in which the believers of Scythopolis met, and the plump woman, Lydia, said she knew someone who might give them permission to use the local edifice. As the crowd left the bakery, the redhead told Barnabas, "Regardless of where we meet tomorrow night, I'm going to bring someone who needs to be here."

Next day, like most of the days in Antioch, sounded like a festival. People enjoyed clowns and musicians who performed along the wide streets. Carefree natives bought their meals from food vendors and ate in the streets, feeding the dogs that crowded about them and pausing for a nap in a public square or along the walkway.

As Barnabas approached the mighty basilica, he could see the red-headed woman standing in front with someone in a brown tunic. As he drew closer, he recognized the protruding teeth and beak-like nose. A serious man stopped Barnabas to inform him that the legal authorities had given written permission for the church to meet in the basilica. While they talked, Thorn Bush walked past them and headed for the man with the long nose. The leather merchant recognized him as the man who had robbed Barnabas, and he swing the anvil of his fist into the thief's face. As Barnabas ran to stop his friend, the victim spit out a mouthful of blood and two front teeth. The wounded man left, cursing Thorn Bush and Barnabas.

The woman with hair the color of copper had deep circles of blue around both eyes, but the swelling had gone down. She said, "He came to hear what was on the parchment." Thorn Bush refused to apologize and left before the service started.

People of Antioch had a custom of giving everyone a nickname. Barnabas couldn't convince them that his name was a nickname, and the catechumens threatened to find him a less serious one.

Barnabas learned that the redheaded girl was a slave

named Rhoda, but they called her Torch. The teacher without a nickname learned that she had duties that kept her from attending his morning classes in a vacant shop next to the bakery on Jawbone Street, a name which led to many jokes among the believers. Some came the first day of classes, others came the second, and all showed up on the third day to be instructed. Barnabas felt like the miser who had wished for gold and then discovered that everything he touched turned to the precious metal.

The teacher felt secure when he taught from the parchment or told of his memories of Stephen. Yet he felt uneasy when some of the synagogue leaders who had become believers began to ask about the Gentiles who had been baptized into the church without becoming Jews first. A handsome youth who had studied philosophy in Athens asked in class, "If Christ is equal to God, then we worship two gods." Barnabas shook his head, but the young man was not satisfied. "If God and Christ are the same, then his death on the cross was not possible."

The teacher looked at the pitifully small parchment in his left hand—just a fragment—and he longed for scrolls that would tell the complete story of Jesus' life. He wished he knew the Torah and wished that he had studied with an authority like Gamaliel.

Whenever Barnabas remembered the events that had brought him to Antioch, he grew discouraged. Feelings of failure now tormented the Son of Encouragement as he headed for the building that was crowded with inquirers, catechumens, and members. After he had recalled how he had come to this place to help, Barnabas watched Lydia and Rhoda, still miffed from their argument, refusing to walk into the basilica together. He and the leather dealer, walking in together, were the last to enter the meeting. Thorn Bush had been a faithful inquirer, missing only a few of the evening services since the Hawk incident. He was even a good adviser, but he still had not joined.

As Barnabas spoke to the large crowd, he wondered if this would be the night that the leather merchant would make his decision. Others decided—but not Thorn Bush.

At the end of the session, Barnabas announced, "I won't be here to teach you tomorrow night." Lydia moaned. She hadn't missed a single night since arriving in the great city. "I will be gone for several weeks."

The redheaded slave girl stood. "My God!" Believers stared at the young woman they had heard curse. She lifted her eyes toward the arched ceiling of the law court. "My God, what will we do?" She sounded as if she were praying.

Barnabas asked the people to get quiet. He moved up to the judge's bench where he could see everyone. "I plan to go for help. If I fail in Tarsus, I'll go to Rome to seek out the new teachers there." He noticed that Rhoda was crying on Lydia's shoulder.

The voyage was as pleasant as a Jewish mother's lullaby. Barnabas walked over the sun-scrubbed deck observing the vessel. The hours of the relatively short trip unraveled themselves in a creeking of timbers and in the swaying of the cradle-like ship.

Barnabas discovered that one of the sailors was from Tarsus. They stood and talked beneath the sky-reaching sail, with its cordage loose, fluffed into a giant, cruising wing. The Cypriot asked if he knew Saul, the tent and sailmaker.

"No, I don't know him." He spat downwind. "He travels

about Cilicia spreading his strange ideas. He likely isn't in Tarsus now." There came a loud cry from the mast, and he said, "They've sighted land. I must get to my station."

Barnabas got his gear together and waited on the deck. A brisk wind pushed the ship toward the harbor. Barnabas watched a small group of people on the dock become clearer in outline. One of the shortest figures there attracted his attention, even though the other people were dressed in brighter robes. His excitement increased like a flame reaching dry leaves. He continued to watch the figure in the camel-colored robe. He decided to wave. The person with a beard returned the wave.

As the ship pulled alongside the wharf and threw lines over to be secured, he relived his former surprise at meeting the short man who had returned with a camel caravan from Damascus, where he had gone on a mission of persecution. He had been amazed that so small a person could have terrified the believers. He felt those same emotions as he fixed his eyes on a man who looked exactly like Saul. He knew if this were the man, he wouldn't have to hire a guide nor stalk Saul's trail to some distant town. His heart pounded faster, with a loud pump. As he recognized Saul's toothfilled smile, he almost wept for joy.

They embraced. Barnabas felt like Jonathan finding David. Then he pushed Saul back in order to look into his eyes and ask, "How did you know to be here?"

"Barnabas," he said in a slow musical way, "last night I dreamed that a ship from Jerusalem would come sailing in, bringing me a part of the scroll of Isaiah. I didn't comprehend the meaning, but I awaited the arrival of this vessel. Why did you come?"

"My brother, my ship didn't come from Jerusalem. I came from Antioch." He picked up his roll of baggage and followed the native of Tarsus past a smelly horse stable. He tried to explain the situation he had left. "I have tried to nurse these babes in Christ, but they need to be weaned. I need your help as a servant of the church."

Saul repeated the phrase *servant of the church.* "You mean Servant of the Lord. Oh, that's the reason I dreamed of Isaiah. The servant is to be a light to the Gentiles. Surely this is God's doing. It is marvelous in our eyes."

After a night of rest in Saul's home, Barnabas doubted that his good fortune would continue. Neither spoke during their breakfast of bread and boiled fish. Then Saul said, "I wonder if I should go."

The doubt in his voice, as different from the previous day's confidence as the snows of Mount Hermon from the salts of Sodom, squeezed a confession out of Barnabas: "I had wanted to do the work alone and report back to Peter and James and the church all that I had accomplished—alone."

"I was in Damascus and Arabia alone."

"Yes, Saul, but was your work as successful as you hoped?"

"No, I have to admit. Something was missing. Teamship, perhaps. But listen to my doubts about Antioch." Saul's eyes widened, and he spoke rapidly. "Have you considered that God might have sent you to go with me to the regions of the West? Except in Rome and here in Tarsus, where else in the Empire can Christ find a Gentile who has heard of him? No one in Athens, Corinth, or Ephesus has heard his name."

The Cypriot dismissed the subject. "God sent me to bring

you to the catechumens of Antioch. You were trained to
work with . . ." Barnabas changed his argument. "If God
wanted you in those places, a man from Athens or Mace-
donia would have come to get you, not me."

Saul went to the window and stared out at the bright new
day. "Years ago I went to Jerusalem for training, because
I wanted the best our religion could offer. My parents, God
grant them rest, could have afforded an education for me in
Athens, but I never seriously considered it. The *Torah* was
more important than philosophy. Permanent and satisfying.
To Jerusalem I went. I observed the methods of the various
teachers within the Temple walls. Most were as rigid as a
Roman arch poured in concrete. But there was one." As Saul
described Gamaliel, Barnabas wondered what Lydia and
Rhoda were doing that morning. Saul reached out the window and picked a grape leaf. "It was while I sat at the feet
of Gamaliel that I dreamed of one day establishing my own
school in Tarsus, for godly young men who couldn't travel
to Jerusalem. From this point, I dreamed that I would send
out dedicated teachers with a new understanding of the
Torah. Then I hoped that one day I would travel to their
synagogues and check on their progress, offering advice and
settling disputes from my storehouse"—he laughed cyni-
cally—"of wisdom."

Barnabas put his hand on Saul's shoulder. "But don't you
see, Saul, this training has equipped you for the present need.
You can train young men in Antioch who will return to their
homes throughout the Empire. Some will go back on grain
ships to Alexandria. Others will return to Rome for marble
building columns. Some will go with caravans to Damascus.
They can take . . . you can give them a better understanding

of Christ than I could. God has prepared you."

Saul closed the window lattice and began to close up the house. He packed his robes and writing materials, and Barnabas wondered what nickname the people in Antioch would give their new teacher.

Two

ALTHOUGH THEY WERE tired out from the voyage, they didn't linger at the fishy-smelling port of Seleucia. Saul was afraid he would be bothered by coastal fevers, so they began the day-long hike from the port to Antioch. They went straight to the inn in the Jewish section. Saul moved in his belongings, and the believers of Antioch gladly paid his lodging. Saul expressed hope that the climate would be healthy.

Barnabus introduced the teacher to the eager pupils, yet they didn't accept Saul as quickly as they had him. He asked a young man with a Greek name about the matter, and he said: "When a beggar reclines at a banquet table, he is so starved that anything tastes good. After he has sampled the main dishes, he becomes more critical of the sweets served at the end."

Barnabas showed Saul what needed to be done, and the teacher from Tarsus willingly accepted every chore. They divided the classes, with Barnabas taking both the inquirers—such as Thorn Bush—and the catechumens preparing for baptism. Saul took the believers who had been baptized already. Lydia never missed a session. The division of labor worked well. Some dropped out of Saul's classes—according to Lydia—because the ideas were becoming more difficult. Barnabas didn't critize but explained to his plump friend that a tree had to be pruned of its dead wood.

Returning to their cubicle at the inn, the roommates began their partnership in a spirit of cooperation. Although some of the Gentiles called him *Paul,* Barnabas stuck with the Hebrew name *Saul.*

One afternoon after Saul had completed his class and returned to their room to study, Barnabas lingered in the classroom to ask about Rhoda. The young man with the Greek name told him that the redhead had been forbidded by her mistress from attending. Then he introduced two of his friends to Barnabas. One with strong shoulders and curly black hair was named Titus. He said, "I really should be in *your* class since I am only an inquirer. But I have a background in philosophy, and I've found that Saul can help me. May I stay?" Barnabas agreed.

The three told Barnabas they had another problem. "Help us find a nickname for Saul."

Barnabas felt uneasy. "That'll be a hard task."

The young men suggested something about his short height or his balding head. Barnabas preferred something about tentmaking, but they couldn't find anything humorous about his occupation.

"I have it. Snaggletooth," said Titus. "The gap between his two front teeth is large enough for another tooth."

The next day Barnabas was standing at the classroom door when the young men tried the name. Saul did not laugh. He took a long time to roll up a scroll of Isaiah. He expressed no anger, but he seemed preoccupied. "I have been called another nickname today." They eagerly asked what it was. "A streetsweeper pointed to me with his broom handle and said, 'You are nothing but a Christian.' The sweeper said *Christian* in a long drawn-out way, hissing on the first syllable like an agitated snake. Some children heard him call me the name and followed me all the way to Jawbone Street singing it after me."

The classroom grew quiet. Titus, who had invented the other name, Snaggletooth, spoke out. "I don't like it. The name is a mockery. It makes the believers sound like a group gathered around a politician, like Caesarians or Pompeians. We don't want to be called Christians."

One said, "I refuse the title." Others nodded their agreement.

Barnabas stepped inside. "I would feel honored to be called a Christian."

Saul's face puffed out and turned pink. "Why?" he demanded.

"A Christian is one who tries to be like Christ, a devoted follower who cannot be convinced of any mistake on his leader's part. It should be no insult to be called a Christian."

Like a hive of disturbed bees, the students buzzed in discussions over the new idea. Despite Saul's reticence, they took the words of Barnabas and repeated them in the marketplace. Pagans laughed, but Christians took the name and began to bear it proudly.

On the day Barnabas learned that Rhoda had run away, Titus was baptized in the river. That night the new convert gave his testimony in the basilica. Barnabas tried to listen but he was worried about the girl's safety and requested a special prayer for her before the benediction.

Barnabas went home with Titus to his handsome villa across from the island of the royal palace. The convert noted his guest's astonishment and said: "Yes, I've received every advantage. I'm grateful my parents provided a *paidagogus* to watch over my early life. He took me to the gymnasium. He forced me to practice my lyre. He carried my books as he daily led me to the academy of the Stoics."

Barnabas ran his hand over the smooth marble of an empty pedestal top. "My life was similar to yours—not with wealth and slaves—but with a yearning for something beyond my home."

Titus said: "Now I want to follow Christ's teaching of perfection. That is why I asked you here. Come." He took Barnabas to the empty kitchen, still smelling of onions and herbs. He showed the Cypriot a sharpened knife. "Use this on me."

Barnabas wondered if the search for truth had so warped the youth's mind that he was thinking of suicide. "What do you mean?"

"I want to be circumcised."

"Do you know what it means?"

"Yes, it is a sacrifice I would gladly make to please God and to surprise Saul. I would gladly sacrifice a part of my body."

"It's more than that."

"I know it would be bloody. Painful. But it's a kind of initiation. A person becomes a member of God's family with this permanent proof. Also it's a health measure."

"Yes, my boy, I believe you understand, but there is one other thing. We must consult Saul. Circumcision is not necessary for salvation. Even now some of the Jews in Jerusalem are insisting that if the good news is carried to Gentiles, they must first come under the knife. But Saul is afraid that such a rule would encourage a salvation by works."

They went to the inn and asked Saul; he didn't take to the idea.

"It is unthinkable."

Titus pled for this symbol of his loyalty. "I am willing."

Barnabas tried to dissuade him. "You would feel intense pain, not like us who were only eight days old and knew no more about losing our foreskins than we did of our umbilical cords. For you it would mean suffering."

Titus said, "I'm not afraid of pain."

Saul glared at Barnabas. "This talk of pain and blood is not the crux of the matter. What really matters is how this would be interpreted—a victory for the strict Jews. No, God has saved you just as he did Abraham, not by sacrifice or circumcision, but by faith. My judgment is this: The rite should not be performed." Barnabas and Titus were silent; they recognized the authority of his argument.

In the following days, more of the believers in Antioch began to seek Saul's advice. The teacher from Tarsus would take a large problem of his students and shrink it as deftly as he might crush a long-legged spider into a tiny wad of matter.

One night Barnabas dreamed of two friends, Sarah and the boy Jacob, trapped in a cistern under the city of Jerusalem. Afterwards, he could not get them out of his thoughts; he wanted to return to check on them. Saul did not like the idea. However, about this same time, some prophets predicted a famine, and the Christians of Antioch decided to send a gift of money to the mother church. They needed honest couriers to take the love offering, and they selected Barnabas and Saul. Barnabas said he was overjoyed that they put that much confidence in one who had come to investigate them. Saul said he would go only if he could take Titus with them. The youth was agreeable, and the three left for Jerusalem.

The trip went quickly, with the trio reaching Caesarea a few nights later. Barnabas wished he could see the Laughing Satyr and his dog once again, but he knew it would sound foolish to say he wanted to see a piece of sculpture.

A guard near the waterfront told them Philip's house was located between the forum and the harbor. Philip, after welcoming them to his house, reported an increasing number of believers in Caesarea. He seemed particularly interested in a centurion named Cornelius. Barnabas regretted that they couldn't stay for the service the next night because of their haste to get to Jerusalem. But they agreed to spend one night in Philip's home. He learned that Rhoda had stayed there on her recent flight to Jerusalem.

A late meal was served by his four daughters, the youngest of whom said she was sixteen. The girl stood by the wall of the dining area and kept her eyes on Titus as he ate.

Something about the gaudy seacoast town reminded Barnabas of Salamis, and he talked about Cyprus. He felt a quiver in his voice and stopped. Saul began to tell about the work in Antioch. The girls had cleared away the dishes and sat on the floor listening. He told about his classes for the advanced. He reported that some of the more eager students were traveling each week to nearby villages. "Titus here has gone as far as the coast to work with the congregation there. Tell them."

In a husky voice, the young man said, "I walk to Seleucia each Friday to hold a service there that night and return home by dawn. I don't claim to be a teacher, but I can pass along what Barnabas and Saul teach me."

After this display of living proof, Saul felt satisfied that his listeners would believe the unusual conversion stories from the Syrian capital. He proceeded to tell about answers to prayer and near miracles. Barnabas noticed that the girls had become more and more enthralled. Then one exclaimed, as if reciting a Psalm, "The Lord has dealt bountifully with you."

Her older sister repeated, "He has dealt mercifully with you."

The youngest said, "He has been a shield and buckler."

The fourth said, "He has delivered you from the mouth of the lion. . . ."

In unison, all four said, "even as Daniel."

Barnabas was amazed. Their remarks sounded like a well-rehearsed Greek chorus. Yet this was no memorized performance.

"He will cause you to speak in strange places."

The one who had stared at Titus said, "He will give you as a light to the Gentiles."

Saul was so overcome with the angel-like message that he bit his lip and lowered his face to the table, covering his head with his arms. His roommate knew it must be an awkward position, but it symbolized his acceptance of the prophetic message.

"You will scatter the gods of Greece."

"Zeus and Aphrodite you will break into pieces."

"You will take God's word to a strange land."

Barnabas felt his scalp contracting in excitement. He thought it strange that God had ordained strength from babes and weaklings.

"He will give you as a light . . ."

". . . a light . . "

". . . a light to the Gentiles."

Saul lifted his palms toward the ceiling and said, "Blessed be the Lord." In a loud, fast whisper, he repeated the words. He got up and marched around the room, like a trumpeter around Jericho. Barnabas felt prickly discomfort and could not keep still. Suddenly, he sprang to his feet and chanted "Blessed be the Lord." The others in the room took up the rhythm and followed in a march of praise.

Above the noise of prancing feet, Saul abbreviated his thought to the simple word "Blessed." He tossed the word and others in the procession threw it back to him. Then a terrifying shriek halted each marching foot. The youngest daughter toppled, quivering, but Titus threw his strong arms under her limp body before it touched the floor. In a relaxed voice, she sighed, "I am happy."

Her words seemed a fitting benediction to the strange events of the evening. Barnabas and Saul took blankets to the arbor-covered roof. Lying there in the coastal breeze, neither could sleep. Barnabas asked, "Have you ever been more thrilled?"

"Yes, on the Damascus Road."

"Did you respond in this way?" Barnabas still was amazed at the responsiveness of the rigid teacher.

"No. Entirely different. I was blind at Damascus. Here I was given insight. Tonight I felt like David before the ark. I lost myself." Barnabas smiled as he thought of the ancient monarch, stripped and ecstatic. "Did I do anything foolish?" Without waiting for an answer, he said, "I caught the spirit of the seers. These girls had what the prophets had seven centuries ago. I caught their fervor."

"And I caught yours."

When Barnabas was almost asleep, Saul spoke. "But there's a danger."

Barnabas was irritated at the change.

"You shouldn't try to repeat it for your own gratification. All things for the Lord should be done decently and in order."

For a long time they listened to the waves pounding against Herod's mighty breakwater. The sloshing was powerful and energetic—yet solemn. Between that house and the beach, there was a jail, used for political prisoners and for some who had appealed to Caesar.

The visitors to Jerusalem went straight to the house of James, where they received a more cordial welcome than they had anticipated. The leader asked if Titus had become a Jew but did not seem perturbed at the negative answer. He was most appreciative of the Antioch gift and requested that Barnabas explain it to the congregation at the upper room.

Barnabas could never ascend the stairway to the upper room without remembering the sight of Ananias and Sapphira being carried down the same steps. Inside, he learned that some of the original Twelve had left the Holy City. He wasn't sure whether all the Seven were still in Jerusalem. He tried to show no surprise at the weakness of his aging aunt, who still presided as a gracious hostess. She, and a group of older women, hugged him.

Sarah was there, more poised than when she had nursed him after his accident. Her complexion was still the color of a delicate sea shell. They smiled at each other but did not touch. She said she hoped that Jacob would come along presently. As Barnabas addressed the meeting, his eyes searched the congregation for the apprentice. During Saul's lengthy talk, he kept watching the door, but it didn't open.

They found the lad back at the pottery, eating dates. Jacob's head came up to Barnabas' shoulder. During a brief embrace, the man wondered if this might be their final one. The boy was getting older and more self-conscious. If persecutions grew worse, he might be butchered along with the more active members. Jacob anticipated his question: "I didn't go to the service tonight; once a week's enough for me."

Barnabas laughed—he could see himself as a boy. He remembered saying the same thing to his mother. Sarah left to get them some goat milk.

"Barnabas, in your travels you've seen a lot of sculpture. Why isn't there more in Jerusalem?"

He tried to answer honestly. "There's a danger of glorifying the human body—even worshiping it."

"Then it's wrong."

Barnabas couldn't give an unqualified yes. His mind spun a web of memories over a piece of sculpture he had known—not just looked at but known—like one knows another person. The Laughing Satyr romped and chuckled before his eyes. "It captures beauty."

"Then statues are all right."

"No. It's not that simple. They must be judged."

"Barnabas, they are either all right or all wrong."

"I wish . . ." He thought of the lad's eye for beauty in ceramics, his hands skilled in a craft—denied this other form of art.

The boy, tall and thin as a hyssop stalk, concluded the argument. "It's all too confusing. Let's drink our milk."

Next day, the three of them lingered over the morning meal. No one mentioned Zadok, for fear of spoiling the reunion with sadness. The boy imitated some of his customers. Sarah threw her head back and laughed toward the ceiling. Barnabas hoped that Jacob would leave for the workshop so he could talk with Sarah. However, a visitor at the door said that Peter and James wanted Barnabas to come to talk with them in the upper room.

The discussions lasted into the afternoon and resumed the next morning. The happiness of the trip was spoiled by a group of rigid leaders who insisted that Titus should be inducted into the Jewish faith. Saul refused, saying that the young man was proof that God could shower the gift of the Spirit on Gentiles. Barnabas did not mention the youth's willingness to submit. The Son of Encouragement suggested that they cut short their visit and return to Antioch. He said farewell to the boy and the young woman. Sarah mentioned a red-haired slave who had passed through Jerusalem that morning on her way to Alexandria. Barnabas wanted to head south, but he already had invited his cousin John Mark to go to Antioch with them.

On the return trip, Barnabas expected Titus and Mark to become close friends because of their ages and common interests. However, Titus walked with Saul, and Mark walked with Barnabas.

John Mark brought several scrolls to Antioch for the teachers to use. Saul borrowed the Isaiah and Psalms scrolls but paid little attention to Mark's own treasure, the life of Jesus.

Barnabas gave him two days time to make use of it, and then he could remain silent no longer. "Don't you want to use Mark's scroll on Jesus, Saul?"

"An apostle speaks from his own familiarity with Christ. I have met the risen Lord. I prefer to speak from my own confrontation."

On the third day as they were returning from the class-room on Jawbone Street, Saul said, "This is the kind of place where you could work the rest of your life."

A jab in the belly couldn't have been any more surprising. Barnabas felt the simple remark awakening him to the unex-pected permanency of the work. He had never wanted to be rooted in one place like a tree. Like an eagle, he hoped to soar from one height to another. He said to his companion: "I don't know how much longer I will remain here. I need to pray."

It was a time for prayer. Saul said he dreaded repercus-sions from Jerusalem, fearful that any day messengers might arrive and demand that the good news be withheld from Gentiles. Several other leaders were concerned about their families or friends. One wealthy Christian was worried over the self-centeredness of the Antioch congregations, which had taken up no gifts since the first collection for famine-stricken Jerusalem. A roomful of men met to pray. They began to talk to their God, each one in turn unveiling his soul. The Cypriot's knees ached from pressing against the floor. Still the prayer continued. The hours wore on, and they didn't stop to eat.

The combination of prayer and fasting produced minds that were receptive to a new idea. Barnabas said, "Someone should take the news to places it hasn't been heard."

Saul said, "Amen! We must spread the message as far as possible before persecution stops us or the Lord returns."

Wealthy Manaen, who had grown up a playmate of Herod Agrippa in Rome, said: "We must use our money on others besides ourselves. I can think of no better investment than to send Christian ambassadors to Cyprus or Crete or Rome."

After each one in the circle had expressed approval, Barnabas and Saul volunteered. Saul added: "When I completed my studies with 'Our Master' Gamaliel, he laid his hands on my head in blessing and sent me forth to serve. The church has the power to do this same thing."

Barnabas suggested Mark as a helper. However, hands were laid on only two heads, those of the "sent ones," Barnabas and Saul. It was understood that Mark would take his own scrolls, instruct new members, watch after the baggage, and act as a secretary to the ambassadors, writing frequent reports back to the church. Immediately after the ordination, the trio started. Barnabas wondered how the trip would end.

Saul said to Mark, "Nothing looks as shabby and smells as bad as a seaport." The sights and smells of Seleucia confirmed his words to the new traveler. The busy street that led down to the wharf was lined with stone buildings that squeezed out much of the light and most of the fresh air. Chicken feathers collected on the edge of a street, while the remainder of a fowl carcass, though not visible, emitted an odor. Dirty children stopped their scampering in the filth to ask the strangers for money. Soon the smell changed to another one, which could be verified by the fish scales that collected like sand in dunes.

The ship they took was an old, leaky vessel, but they were concerned only for their mission. Immediately on leaving the harbor, the gentle swells started. The craft pushed aside foam and dashed spray into the air. Mark grew seasick. Lying on the deck and looking up, he said, "The mast looks as if it's scraping the sky." The boat gave a feeling of dropping into holes, and he said nothing else.

Barnabas looked over the rail. He watched blue-gray clouds veiling the sun. Radiating beams, both up and down, were cast from behind the clouds. The Cypriot, heading westward toward his home, felt close to his Creator.

After nightfall, the creeks and sighs of the ship became more noticeable. There was a large moon somewhere behind the clouds, and it threw a patch of white far out on the surface of the sea. Barnabas could almost hear a Roman soldier calling it *our* sea.

Nothing at the venerable harbor of Salamis interested Barnabas. He felt pulled toward the western edge of the city to the little house where his mother lived. He left Saul and Mark to inquire at the forum, and he began the hot walk through pushing crowds.

Her vats were boiling that day, and two well-fed girls were helping his mother, poking the steaming cloth. She looked wrinkled, just as she had when he left fifteen years before. There was no room on that face for new wrinkles.

He didn't want to shock her with his abrupt appearance and called to one of the girls to come and take a message. He watched the matriarch solemnly receive the word, leave her thriving little industry, and point him to the house. She walked more slowly than he remembered, but she showed no emotion. Once inside the house, the springs of joy gushed forth. "My son, Joseph." She hugged him. "My son."

Through the choking in his throat, Barnabas pushed some

words. "It is good to be home again. You are looking just the same." He smelled the faint odor of onion on her breath, and he felt happy.

"Joseph," she said urgently, "are you well?"

"Yes, dear one. My hair is beginning to change its color. But, after all, I am thirty-nine years old."

"You eat Mama's cooking awhile, and you hair will change back. The Lord is good to send you back to me."

Barnabas had planned to wait until later—after an ample Cyprus meal—to talk about his new life. Earlier, he had intended to write her about his great change, but he was never as gifted as Saul in putting ideas into writing. He had waited for an opportunity of unhurried explanation. If he delayed, she would assume that he had come back to work with her in the dyeing business. She would think that he had returned to live. He must tell her now.

"I have learned that the Messiah has come."

"Are you sure that this is not just another leader trying to rebel against Rome?" Her son nodded. "Where is he now?" She asked the question enthusiastically, as if ready to believe.

"He was killed on the cross at Jerusalem."

She sighed. As he continued, she showed a polite interest. Yet there was a puzzled line that remained on her forehead. She could not grasp what had happened to his thinking. Finally, she shook her head and said: "I do not understand all this servant idea and resurrection story. I am interested because you are interested. Right now, let us think of eating."

He was not conscious of any taste except garlic, although he was pleased to sit again at his mother's table. After the meal, they lingered. She asked about her sister in Jerusalem and was amazed that she, too, had become a believer. As his mother blinked her eyes in unbelief, he tried to answer her questions. He did everything he could to present the life of Christ clearly, and yet she could not understand. "Joseph, you are tired from travel. Get some rest now. We will speak of this again."

They did not get to converse about the Messiah the next day. She arose early to deliver some dyed pieces to a tailor. Barnabas went to the marketplace and found Saul talking to a tentmaker. As the weaver threw his shuttle and brought it back, Barnabas learned from this Christian craftsman that one of the synagogues had become a haven for believers, with even the rabbi accepting the Way. "Another synagogue, House of Israel, is opposed to any Christian teaching."

"That is the one I attended from childhood."

"There is not a believer in the congregation."

Barnabas inquired about various people. Some had died and others had moved to Paphos or Antioch. Then he recalled the child, Rufus, who accompanied him to the docks when he left. "Where could I find the boy now?"

The tentmaker said, "At the gymnasium," and continued weaving.

Barnabas showed Saul the way to the believers synagogue, and he went on to the gymnasium of Salamis. Even though it had been fifteen years since he left the city, he figured it had been about twenty-one since he had been carefree enough to visit the place of the athletes. He entered and walked past column after column. He observed how the place had been beautified. The basic plan was still the same, but it was more ornate. It contained almost as many columns as the Jerusalem Temple, but these were more delicately carved. The shafts were more gracefully ribbed and the entablature more decorated. He discovered mosaics on the bathhouse floor and marble flagstones on the promenade.

The doorkeeper, a dark-skinned slave, told him he could find Rufus in the inner court, preparing for a wrestling bout. As he went in he sensed an excitement that a trained athlete can recognize, like a musician feels when he hears an orchestra tuning up. Some of the young men in the gymnasium had stopped other pursuits of racing and throwing. They had thrown towels and robes over their bodies to absorb the sweat. Others had come in from the street, wearing tunics and togas. Barnabas wondered if he looked conspicuous in his heavy travel clothing.

The gymnasiarch called the two opponents from their training areas, where they had been performing squatting exercises. For their warm-ups, they were wearing garments as heavy as his but of a lighter color.

Barnabas had no clue as to the identity of Rufus. He tried to picture the five-year-old child who had helped him pack and who had played with the gold pieces that he later gave the church.

At a signal, they stripped and left their clothing with the assistants. The hairy-chested one was not a Jew. He knew the other one must be Rufus. The two youths stood facing each other within a large circle, like two wild animals ready to pounce. They began a slow circling dance, with hands outstretched. Their bodies were tight and disciplined, with no lazy flabbiness or childish fat. He noticed the developed muscles that flared from their backs to their shoulders. Their physiques were taut, like the stretched main timber of a catapult.

Suddenly, they grabbed each other by the arms, and the match had begun. Each man was still on his feet, pushing with his head into the right shoulder of his opponent. They were equally matched in weight, and presumably, in strength.

After the opening tie-up, they broke clean and came at each other again. One of the spectators yelled, "Watch out, Rufus," as the hairy wrestler came toward his opponent with an attempted leg tackle. Rufus whipped back his legs and arched his back, leaning against the other man's shoulders. Then he spun behind him and took his opponent off his feet.

Rufus was riding on top of the other youth. It seemed that for a long time nothing happened. The gymnasiarch dropped to his hands and knees to see if Rufus had the man's shoulders pinned to the ground. There was a sudden twist, and their positions were reversed. Rufus arched his back, panting and struggling to keep his shoulders from being pinned down.

A quick movement helped Rufus escape control, and he was on his feet instantly. He lunged for his opponent's waist and carried him down. From that time on, the match belonged to Rufus. He restricted any free movement of the wrestler with the matted chest hair. Then he executed a pinhold, completing the match with his adversary's shoulders resting firmly on the ground.

When the fight was over, both stood, gasping and looking confused. The official came forward and held up Rufus' hand in victory. The spectators cheered, congratulated him, and then went off to watch other events.

Barnabas went to the champion. They were the same

height, but Barnabas realized that he had allowed himself to grow a little paunchy. He looked at the younger man and saw droplets of water running off his head down his entire body.

"I am Joseph. I have been in Jerusalem." He had not used his old name in years, and it brought back strange echoes of his former life of taverns and wrestling rings. Waiting for the young athlete's response, Barnabas' heart pounded.

"Jerusalem is a great distance from Salamis," said a voice that was deep but unfriendly.

"I wonder if you remember me." He tried not to appear too anxious.

"Yes, I remember. I used to cry myself to sleep wishing you would come back. I never heard from you, and I tried to forget you."

"I have come back. I made the most marvelous discovery in Jerusalem. I want to share it with you."

"You have come back too late." The words were as mournful as if they had been a prayer for the dead. Barnabas received no encouragement to continue the conversation. The wrestler stood there, still perspiring. He covered his glistening body with a sheet that reminded Barnabas of his own baptismal garment.

"I've learned something from you." Barnabas said without sarcasm. "I cannot pick up the clay I dropped fifteen years earlier and mold the same vessel."

With no emotion, Rufus said, "Farewell, Joseph." He turned and walked proudly toward the steam room, trailing a corner of the sheet along the marble promenade.

Barnabas commanded his mind to think of something —anything except the heartbreaking loss. Returning to this place had been like seeing a moving statue of himself. Twenty-one years before he had been proud of his body and unworried with matters of philosophy and religion. Breaking away from the yoke of the law, he had been one of the few Jewish boys to frequent the pagan gymnasium. Most of his friends had strict fathers who would not allow such close association with Gentiles. In contrast, he knew how to talk his trusting mother into giving her permission. She seemed to have no fear of non-Jews.

Out on the street, tears splashed on to the hot cobblestones, as he went to see if Saul had had more success in his attempts. Barnabas found the teacher from Tarsus sitting in front of the stone synagogue with an old farmer. The sky was yellowish.

The farmer said, "I hope your visit will bring some luck to our island. Past time for the rains."

"Are they much later this year?" asked Saul.

"Latest in years. The proconsul has sent word that he will import grain if we have a famine."

"He sounds like a good man," said Barnabas.

"Sergius Paulus is like a father to us. But I hope we won't need his help. My seeds have been planted many days now. They lie there in the ground, waiting for a drink of water."

Barnabas' head began to hurt, and he told the men he had to go to lie down. Saul said, "If you get to feeling better, come to the House of Israel tonight. I have arranged a meeting with the rabbi and a few elders."

More than anything else, Barnabas wanted to return to his old synagogue, but the throbbing pain in his head grew worse with every step home. He knew it would take a miracle for him to get to the conference.

By the time he reached the house, he began to feel nauseated. His head hurt so much that he could not tell if he actually heard thunder or just a roaring in his ears. He awoke. He heard the shrieking of the wind and the pelting of large drops of rain against the side of the house. He felt secure in the sturdy house, and he knew his mother in the next room was all right. He began to think about the people in the town who were without belief and wondered what their superstitious fear of storms might make them do. He recalled rumors of the Emperor in Rome crouching under his bed, trembling and crying during a storm.

A tapping at the front door awakened him the next morning. It was Saul, who said, "We must change our plans."

Barnabas pulled his robe about him and stepped out into the early morning light and saw there rotten eggs broken against the side of the house and across the front door. They had not been there the night before, or the rain would have washed them away. They had just been thrown. He noticed a few people moving up and down the street.

Back inside they found that the industrious little woman had awakened and had begun making a fire for the morning meal. She bent over her work, oblivious to the stranger who had come in. When her son told her that this was Saul of Tarsus, she smiled and said warmly, "Welcome, my son."

They heard a banging at the front door and moved toward it. Barnabas and Saul, expecting some sort of trouble, moved ahead of the woman and planned to take care of the situation. They expected to see a crowd gathered in the doorway, but when they opened it they saw only a large bearded man. A few other people were scattered across the street and away from the house. "I want to see the dye woman. I have come from the rabbi," he said.

"It is my joy to hear from the teacher of the Law."

The big man stood in the doorway, refusing to come in. He had a protruding stomach, and his thick neck was drawn straight up and back so that he looked down at her. He had a short upper lip and a protruding lower one that left a permanent haughtiness on his face. "You are responsible for what happened to our synagogue last night."

Barnabas interrupted, "She was here all night long."

"She has contaminated herself by associating with you two unclean deserters of the Law. The storm last night blew in the roof of the synagogue. The rain put out the eternal light. All furnishings were ruined. Only the locked up scrolls were saved from damage." Frowning people began to close in behind the messenger and peer into the house.

Barnabas yelled: "Stop. Stop talking to her in this manner. She had nothing to do with your accident." He was sorry he had said *your.* He sensed Saul edging close to him to give protection.

The lofty man's voice became more gruff. "You have contaminated yourself. You cannot return to the synagogue until you go through a period of purification." With this, he spat on her door.

Barnabas felt his face getting hot. He clinched his teeth and moved toward the man until he was stopped. Saul's strong arms grasped him from the rear. "Let me go," he hissed.

Saul talked to him as if he were gentling a wild horse. "No, Barnabas. Calm down, Barnabas. Steady now." The door became empty except for the curiosity seekers who still looked in, sneering.

"Let me stop that fool. He insulted Mama." Barnabus knew that Saul had never before seen him so enraged. Barnabas struggled loose from the tight grip of his friend. He was ready to fight.

The frail woman stopped him. She closed her spittle-dripped door and stood in front of it. "Joseph, people will always look for a scapegoat." She stood for a long moment, staring at the hearth. Her face was wrinkled. "This will hurt my business. Son, you must leave. Do not come here anymore. You are my son regardless of what religion you profess, but your coming will make life harder for me. I cannot afford it. Leave."

He had never heard his mother talk so selfishly. She was a resentful old woman, peeved because of his going to Jerusalem and now disapproving of his new religious belief. He could not understand her interest in money and reputation.

It was time when many things needed to be said. Yet no one broke the fragile silence. Barnabas picked up his things and moved toward the door. A tear had appeared on the wrinkled cheek of the woman, and the same puzzled look that had been there the night before returned. Saul said nothing but bowed to her as he would have to an empress. Barnabas knew that under any other circumstances his companion would have tried to persuade such an individual to accept the Messiah, but now he did not speak. As the door closed, Barnabas knew that another part of his life was over. Incomplete, yes, but over—his life was a banquet interrupted before the main course was served.

The travelers circled by the house of Mnason for Mark and their baggage. They ran out the southwest road from the city. Even though his life was in danger, Barnabas considered turning back and running to Rufus and to his mother. Paul advised him not to misjudge his mother's words. After they came to open country along the coastal road, they began to feel somewhat safe. They traveled around the southern shore of the island, stopping at villages that had existed since Phoenician times. Barnabas couldn't speak of the joy of the Christian life. He let Saul do the talking.

"We are a religious people," a pottery craftsman bragged to Saul. He was referring to a contented paganism, practiced from the temple of Zeus at Salamis to the temple of Aphrodite at Paphos. In between these eastern and western extremities, there were temples to Apollo, Artemis, and others. Devotees dared anyone to tamper with their beliefs. Their lives—full of lust and revenge—were governed by the flight of a bird, an appearance of an animal's liver, or the position of the stars.

After many disappointing days, they passed the shambles of Old Paphos, which had been damaged by an earthquake more than fifty years before, and they came to New Paphos, the capital. They found lodging at the home of Mnason's brother.

The next day they left Mark, writing and studying, and they spent the morning talking with people at the marketplace. When they started for the house of Mnason's brother, they found traveling difficult. It was like swimming upstream as Saul and Barnabas pushed their way through the busy street of people, all of whom were going in the opposite direction. It seemed that everyone in Paphos that day was heading for the arena. Workers had closed up shops. Slaves must have been given the afternoon off. All of Paphos was being provided a holiday spectacle by some wealthy politician who wanted votes. Barnabas realized that the crowd was thinning out a bit. Then there was a space. Next he saw eight Roman soldiers with metal helmets and breastplates gleaming. They seemed to be body guards. Behind them walked a tall man in a magnificent white Roman toga trimmed in purple. His thin, sandy hair grew forward covering half his brow. He looked like a statue of the Emperor Augustus come back to life. The soldiers stepped aside and Barnabas found himself looking squarely into the face of this important personage. With eyes the color of the sky, he stared at Barnabas and then looked at Saul. He spoke, "Citizens, you are heading in the wrong direction. You will never reach the arena this way."

"We know. We are not heading for the arena. We are going to a friend's house for rest." Barnabas was not intimidated.

The man in the toga asked, "I wonder if you know who I am?"

Saul spoke. "Could you be the proconsul of this island?"

"You have guessed rightly. I am Sergius Paulus. A close friend of mind, Gamba, is giving the gladiatorial games today, and I feel it is a bad omen for citizens to refuse attendance."

Barnabas looked down at his friend and wondered what answer he would give. The apostle answered, "I am not a citizen of this town. Like you, I am a Roman citizen. My name is also the same as yours, although I am called Saul of Tarsus. My friend, Barnabas, and I do not have a permanent home on this earth. Our temporary headquarters is Antioch of Syria."

The official sensed there was something unusual about

these two, and he chanced being late for the games to ask them further questions. "You speak as if you fear no man on earth. Even though you are not from this vicinity, let me invite you to join my party and attend the games."

Barnabas was quick to respond. He was afraid that Saul might react with a blunt statement that would jeopardize their freedom. "Sir, we are deeply honored. However, we have other interests at this time."

"What could be more interesting than gladiators?"

Saul answered, "We believe from the law of Moses that killing is wrong. So we do not care to watch two men break the law until a life is thrown away."

"But this is not murder." The statement came from just behind Sergius Paulus. The speaker was a young man who wore a meticulously white toga, without any color on its border. His hair was black and curly, looking as if it had been waved. He had a Semitic look, although his lips were thin and expressive. Except where his shaved beard showed through his skin, he looked like a beautiful woman.

The proconsul introduced them to the speaker. "This is Elymas Bar-Jesus. He is an authority on world religions."

"The *Torah* states that you shall do no murder." Barnabas sensed that the speaker, Elymas, was a Jew by birth. "That means premeditated, wilful murder. Since the gladiators fight not out of anger but out of sport, there is nothing unlawful about the games." Elymas pointed out to the proconsul the thinning crowd and the approaching time for the events to start.

Sergius Paulus said to the strangers: "Go your way, but, Paul, you and your assistant come to my palace tomorrow at this same time. I want to find out more about your idea of the Law." His soldiers marched forward, and the governor and his retinue soon disappeared down the street.

Early the next afternoon the friends, full of hope, started toward the palace. Barnabas said: "Few people on the streets. Probably resting from the heat of the day. A contrast to yesterday afternoon. Saul, this is one of the most pagan cities I have ever seen."

"It takes religion less seriously than Antioch. If there is a synagogue here, I haven't seen it."

"No one tries to live righteously. I understand that girls still celebrate the birth of Aphrodite by offering themselves on the beaches every . . ."

"Barnabas, we must do everything we can to win some people here before moving on." He stared at his companion. "Please, don't call me Saul any longer."

"I'm sure I'll forget. You can't change a habit overnight."

"If you set your mind to it, you can. It would not matter what you call me in private, but in public, try to remember. I want nothing as insignificant as a Hebrew name to separate me from the Gentiles I hope to win."

"Very well, *Paul.*" Barnabas said the name with a tone of resignation and with a hint of a smile at the corner of his lips.

The palace was situated in the southern part of New Paphos. They had passed it on their first afternoon in the city. It not only was a residence, but a fortress as well. As they came near, they looked down the street that circumscribed the walls and saw the proconsul. They paused, surprised that he was out walking his horse in the noonday sun of a bright winter's day, and watched him move in their direction. He had a proud bearing. He stopped to inspect a paving stone that had broken. Barnabas knew that this man expected the best in construction. He formerly had been Curator of the Tiber, a responsible position in Rome's architectural and commercial life.

When he reached the pair, he did an unusual thing. An ordinary person would have spoken and inquired about their health. This patrician, accustomed to associating with royalty and picking up some of their eccentricities, made an introduction. "This is Rex." He pointed to a fine horse, from which he had just dismounted, and it was led by a guard holding the tether. "We people of Cyprus value a good horse. Years ago leaders used to decree that their horses be buried with them in the entranceway to their tombs. No one in recent years has even considered such a waste of power."

A slave, called a *nomenclator,* performed his job of recalling names and whispered something to his master. The great man said, "Rex, I want to present Paul and Barnabas."

Barnabas was not as surprised to hear the introduction as to hear his name used last. He knew that they were expected to speak to the horse, but he guessed that Paul would never bring himself to enter into such foolishness. So he patted the stallion above its nose and addressed the proconsul, "You were fortunate to find such a fine animal to become a member of your household."

Barnabas had said exactly the right thing. The governor was pleased and asked them to enter the palace grounds. Guards let them enter the gate, and they walked across the pavement that had been laid out in a severe geometric design. Sergius Paulus sent his attendants with Rex to the stables. He said to the two visitors, "Come with me."

They expected to ascend the stairs to the main entrance

and then, perhaps, to a formal audience room. But the unpredictable Roman took them down a half-flight to his *tepidarium*. This wealthy official had his own steam room, complete with Roman baths, both warm and hot. They entered an anteroom, where a slave helped him disrobe. Saul instinctively looked in another direction. Even though some Jews in Jerusalem had responded to the trends of hellenization, and even a few had participated in public games naked, most of them abhorred the idea of nudity in public sporting events. Romans, on the contrary, had enveloped the Greek idea of the body beautiful in sculpture and sports.

Sergius Paulus invited them to join him in the baths. They graciously refused and waited uncomfortably in the tiny anteroom. The delicate young man, Elymas, the authority on religion, came into the room. He directed a slave who carried a fresh tunic and toga. Elymas spoke hospitably. They inquired about his length of residence in the palace. "Sergius Paulus is my patron. I have enjoyed this relationship for six months now."

Barnabas responded, "The proconsul is certainly an impressive person. I should think it would be a privilege to be part of his household."

Paul was more blunt. "What do you do?"

Elymas smiled. "I advise him on the movement of the stars. Most intelligent people realize that circumstances are beyond our control but governed by the stars. The science of astrology teaches one how to adjust to these conditions. I am glad to offer him the results of my years of study." He looked to be in his late twenties but sounded older because of his authoritative tone. Then he changed the subject before they could respond. He wondered if they had any news of the disturbance in the Jewish settlement of Salamis. All three knew that considerable unrest existed among the Jewish communities of the island. With oppressive leadership or with new factions, the unrest could erupt into something catastrophic.

Elymas said, "It takes many races to make up the world. Every person is just a tiny grain of sand in this vast beach of the Roman empire. We are insignificant. Just playthings of fate. This world should be a place of pleasure. Some have made it a hostile, alien place simply to be endured. Nevertheless, no afterlife follows it."

Paul said, "How can you be so fatalistic? Doesn't your common sense teach you that God made this world and your life? He doesn't expect to throw either of them away. He'll take care of what he has created."

"Everything that happens in this lower world is determined by what goes on in the world of the stars. We are under their control. I wouldn't think of starting a day without my horoscope."

Barnabas felt compelled to ask, "How have you strayed so far from the teachings of the *Torah?*"

"My father believed in the *Torah.*" Elymas dug his hand into a money bag that hung at his waist. "He was a cruel man. If I made the slightest mistake, he beat me mercilessly. When he died, I became a happier child and forsook his *Torah.* Now I have discovered that the stars control our destinies. We can't resist fate. Augustus, great man that he was, knew that truth—look at this coin he had minted." They examined the tiny piece of metal he handed them from his bag. It was inscribed with the sign of Augustus' birth, Capricorn. "Emperor Tiberius had an astrologer named

Thresyllus."

Suddenly Sergius Paulus reappeared, draped in a towel. "Come, let us all go to the massage room."

Since they had refused his hospitality of the baths, Barnabas and Paul felt they must accompany him and the heretical Jew to the massage room. It was larger than the anteroom but flooded with light from several window wells.

The official crawled up on one of the marble slabs in the middle. He lay on his stomach, and a Syrian slave, who had bowed low as they entered, started kneeding the proconsul's shoulders. Sergius Paulus sighed. "Some people are austere all the time. Not the Romans—we know how to relax. There are times to be austere and times to be relaxed. Only in this way can we achieve harmony."

Barnabas and Paul did not interupt his rhapsodizing. Then they heard a different topic, one that demanded a response. "You ruined the games for me yesterday."

"I am truly sorry," said Barnabas.

Paul inquired, "How was that possible?"

"We've all grown used to two gladiators fighting until one is killed. Yesterday was supposed to have been more exciting than usual. Female slaves from Gaul were turned loose to fight armed dwarfs." He propped up on his elbows to look his guests in the eyes. "It was the most brutal exhibition I have ever seen. But that bloodthirsty crowd loved it. They were a pack of wild dogs, urging the dwarfs on, screaming for blood." He bit his fist. "It was terrible."

Elymas stepped up to the slab and patted his shoulder in a maternal way. "Don't worry about that. Yesterday the stars were against the victims. You have more important things to occupy your mind."

Barnabas knew Paul shared his uneasy feeling. They were out of place. Both remained silent, like boats being pulled down a river by a strong, noiseless current.

"I've heard of you two before. That's enough for my shoulders—rub my legs now. I get regular reports from over this entire island. You created quite a stir in Salamis."

Barnabas said, "We were misunderstood there."

"It's surprising your own people didn't understand. You offered them something different. The world needs more religions. In Rome, they have begun to talk of building a pantheon. In a different way, we welcome all the gods to Cyprus. One condition remains—you must do nothing to weaken our loyalty to Rome. We can tolerate any religion except one that is subversive."

"Master," Elymas interrupted, "the slaves have prepared a drama for you." This fretful young man seemed better at changing the subject than at any other skill.

Paul said, "We cannot stay, but I am eager to tell you of the faith that we have proclaimed over your island. It will never interfere with one's patriotism, as long as Rome does not extend its demands too far."

"I wish to hear more of this. Come tomorrow at this same time."

They walked across the scrubbed courtyard without speaking. Barnabas believed they were failing. He felt dizzy, but his main concern centered on the turncoat, the *meshumed* Jew. He wanted to put his arm around him, as he would Jacob, and ask him to change his ways.

John Mark had not been with the two travelers. He had developed a fever shortly after leaving Salamis and had not felt like going out with the men each day. He rested and studied his scrolls. Paul expressed suspicion of the continuing weakness and suggested to Barnabas that his cousin might be malingering.

When they reached the home of their host, Mark was not there. Barnabas became alarmed. Paul responded with a grin that showed every front tooth and the space in between. Within a few minutes Mark returned from the marketplace. Underneath his robe he carried a valuable scroll that he had bought in a bookstall. Barnabas shared his enthusiasm, but Paul didn't. "So you are not well enough to help spread the good news but able to go bargain hunting at the bazaars." He sounded more bitter than Barnabas had remembered. "We shall expect you to accompany us tomorrow."

The three of them slept on separate cots in the same room. Barnabas noticed that Paul rolled from one side to the other. Every time he woke up he heard Paul's restless movements. Later in the night he awoke to hear a gurgling sound.

"Yes, yes," Paul was whispering. Then his voice grew louder. Barnabas sensed that Mark was sitting up in his cot. By this time Barnabas' feet were on the floor. Paul began to shout at the top of his voice, "Yes, yes, yes." Barnabas stepped over to him and caught him by the shoulders.

"Wake up, brother." He felt Paul's body trembling.

"I was not dreaming. The Lord was speaking to me in a vision."

Mark spoke for the first time. "Thanks be to Christ. He is doing it again." In those few words he expressed the deep longing in his own life for the early miraculous days after the resurrection. He had never mentioned the recent drabness and failures to his cousin, but Barnabas knew how the youth longed for the golden days of the early Way.

Barnabas said kindly, "Can you share it with us, Paul?"

"It was too terrible to inflict upon anyone else. But I can tell you the end is coming. Christ asked me if I would warn the whoremongers and effeminate, the liars and murderers. I promised him I would start in the morning."

Barnabas couldn't go back to sleep. He was positive that Paul spent the remainder of the night on his knees.

Next morning Paul refused to eat anything which the host offered. Both Barnabas and Mark ate little; they felt uneasy, as if they were setting out a voyage in a leaking boat. When they had completed their meal, Paul herded them toward the heart of Paphos. He was a modern Jonah, speaking to a new Nineveh. The intensity of his voice caused a crowd to gather. He gave one message in the forum and another by the vegetable stalls. He promised to return to both places the next day if the Lord spared any of them.

Barnabas thought he was prepared to understand the many moods of his complex companion, but he remained mystified at the change in Paul's methods. Barnabas began to worry about what might happen if the proconsul became offended by this messenger of doom, but he did not dare to quench the fire which he believed that God had lighted in the mouth of his friend.

The afternoon was warm for a winter day. By the time the three had walked to the palace, Barnabas was sweaty and tired and might have welcomed a bath. He knew that weakened Mark must be exhausted. Paul gave no hint of any letup in his gait. Before they entered the gateway, he turned to Mark. "Remember this is God's work. Say nothing to interfere with my message." He was a teacher scolding a naughty pupil.

A slave took them up the entrance steps of the palace and up an inside flight of stairs. He made a turn and brought them out on a covered porch that faced the sea. There were four curved stone benches on the porch, arranged in a large circle. Sergius Paulus was sitting on one, and each of the three guests chose one. Elymas came out, holding a cat in his arms. Barnabas, who had never touched a cat because of their association with the idolatries of Egypt, watched in fascination, but Paul turned his eyes away.

Behind the stargazer came several slaves. One brought cool, moist grapes. Another carried silver chalices of nectar on a tray. Others had unneeded fans made of dried palms. When the servant who had brought the drinks was leaving the porch, Elymas placed the cat on his empty tray and kissed it good-by. Then the astrologer went over to his master and whispered some information. During the interruption, Mark leaned over to Barnabas and said, "He is older than I expected." For the first time, Barnabas realized that Sergius Paulus must be in his late thirties, perhaps near his own age of thirty-nine. When Elymas completed his secret conversation, he walked over and sat on the same bench with John Mark.

Sergius Paulus began the conversation with an earnestness that surprised Barnabas. "Some of my wealthy friends have turned to excessive drinking and other indulgences. My life is different—yet I am unhappy. You might think of me as one could buy anything. Why do I feel poor?"

Paul said, "You have had material blessings, but they are not all in life. Indeed, this life is not all."

"Exactly right. This is what concerns me. I am not especially interested in sensuous pleasure." Elymas coughed. Sergius Paulus waited. "I have some wealth, yet it can't purchase contentment. I have power to command troops and a will firm enough to rule this island, but this power brings great responsibility. I feel like a father with many—far too many—children. I need help."

Paul was encouraged. "Have you heard about redemption?"

"Yes, I heard of finding immortal life by attending a play."

Barnabas was puzzled, but Paul seemed to comprehend. "Are you speaking of the Eleusinian mysteries?"

"Yes. I have heard on reliable authority that one can make a pilgrimage to the drama site in Greece and there be inducted into the mysteries. I know that the drama concerns the annual death and rebirth of the plant world, but it surely goes much deeper. Everyone who participates must take an oath never to divulge the nature of the event. I've questioned them. They won't tell—but they come away different people.

Elymas said, "Will you convince him that this is just superstition?"

Cautiously, Paul said, "He is talking about a universal hunger in the heart of mankind. All of us want to know that we will live beyond this present life. But this . . ."

"I certainly don't care to," Elymas said. "There is enough trouble in this world. If it were not for guidance from the stars, we could never get through life. I would hate to live forever. I believe in enjoyment now." He batted his eyes in a slow, effeminate way.

Paul sounded angry. "Only a fool is content with this life."

The astrologer said, "Only a fool would believe in myths of an afterlife."

The proconsul seemed changed in mood. "Let's not argue

over these matters. Why not listen to some musicians who are waiting to play on their flutes for us?"

Paul said, "No. I would like to talk about eternal life."

Sergius Paulus shrugged his shoulders. "Proceed, then."

"I sense in you a spark of interest that can be fanned into a flame of salvation. God has put within your heart a yearning for his assurance of his forgiveness and fellowship. There is nothing you can do to earn his favor, by sacrificing or by good works."

Elymas said sarcastically, "I have never heard a rabbi talk like that. Where did you get this teaching, make it up?"

Paul whispered, "Such grace from God offends human logic. We long to wound ourselves, physically or emotionally, to earn his favor. But he gives us this favor, regardless. You can know God and understand him through his Son whom he sent to us. His name is Jesus."

Elymas sneered, "My father had the same name."

Sergius Paulus said, "What on earth are you getting at?"

Barnabas began to pray silently that Paul would become more effective in his presentation. Elymas was making himself more obnoxious all the time. The governor seemed to have only a slight interest. Paul said: "Jesus of Galilee and Judea lived a perfect life. He taught a rule of love. He was misunderstood by our religious leaders, and they encouraged your Roman soldiers to crucify him. We are all responsible for his death."

"I don't understand, but continue."

"He died, asking forgiveness for the ones immediately responsible but bringing salvation to all the world through this supreme sacrifice that was offered. Now his death was not all. After three days this same Jesus was raised from the dead. He appeared to many witnesses who are still living and can testify to the fact."

Sergius Paulus leaned forward, showing more interest. Elymas appeared alarmed. He seemed to be fighting for his life and said, "Don't listen to this idiocy."

The ruler commanded him to keep quiet. Elymas, sensing the desperate situation, turned to his oddest distraction yet. He had tried coughing, sarcasm, dispute, and ridicule. He now began to tease a ravel on the sleeve of the robe worn by John Mark, whose face turned a dark pink. The youth inched away, but Elymas followed him, sitting very close. Barnabas, thoroughly disgusted, was just getting ready to move over and stop the offensive action, when Paul saw what was taking place. The tranquility of the pleasant afternoon was shattered with a roar from the apostle, "Stop this abomination."

Mark, who had hoped not to offend Paul with any distraction, said, "I did nothing to encourage this."

Sergius Paulus said: "There is nothing more beautiful than the love of two equally educated men for the truth and for each other, as our philosophers have taught. Personally, I don't know enough about the subject to agree or disagree. But Elymas, this exhibition with a stranger is disorderly." Barnabas would have preferred his use of the word *disgusting,* but to the Roman *disorderly* was a serious accusation.

Elymas, like a deer at bay, began to lose his composure. "I have given you advice. I have provided your horoscope daily. I have been a companion. And the only reward I have gained is for you to listen to these fanatics."

The proconsul did not appear moved. "You have done what you were expected, and you have my gratitude for your work. My mind now turns to thoughts of a different kind."

Paul folded his arms and bowed his head. Barnabas said to his host, "I hope you will find happiness." The tense situation seemed to be easing.

Sergius Paulus told Elymas he could go. But Paul screamed, "Not yet." The apostle stood up and pointed a long finger that bore scars from tentmaking needles. "There was something about you that I didn't like from the first moment I saw you. I couldn't figure what it was. Now I know." He paused. No one uttered a word. Barnabas noticed a twitch in the astrologer's neck and about his jawbone. He looked like a different person. The attractiveness had vanished from his face; he seemed as hideous as a leper. Paul continued, starting with a low whisper and moving quickly toward a shout, "I know what is wrong. God has given you up to Satan. You are blind to God's laws. You are blind to his good gifts. You are blind to righteousness. You are blind, blind, blind."

During this crescendo of malediction, Elymas dropped to his knees. He said over and over, "No, no." Then he began to sob and moan. Sergius Paulus stood up, excited. Then Elymas let out a shriek, like that of a woman who witnesses the death of her only child. "O God, it is true. I *am* blind. I can see nothing. Who will lead me?" He fell back to the floor sobbing.

The flames of Paul's anger had been fed with new oil. He stood over Elymas, condemning, Barnabas imagined, in a similar way to his searching out the early church members for persecution. His tongue was a blazing torch. "You are not a son of Jesus; you are a son of Satan. You are full of guile and treachery." The pitiful wretch on the floor continued to moan. Then Paul resumed his chant at a lower pitch. "Judgment has come to this place today. Prepare, O judge of men, Sergius Paulus, also to meet your Judge."

Barnabas saw a strange sight. The proconsul went to Paul and took his hand, grasping it in both of his. "I have come to the end of my search."

Slaves led Elymas away whimpering. Paul, now delivered of his message, dropped to a bench in the afterbirth of exhaustion. "I must return to my room and pray for this household."

When he walked out to the stairway, Barnabas lingered with Sergius Paulus and expressed his happiness at the official's decision. The response he heard stuck in his memory. "I am willing to try any religion that can lead me out of this darkness. I plan to give Christ a chance if he work miracles like this. If he can't work others, then I will try another belief." Barnabas chose not to worry Paul with the tenuousness of the new convert's faith and decided to keep quiet.

Sergius Paulus said to the departing Barnabas and Mark, "What will happen to Elymas?"

"Paul pronounced the same judgment that he once received himself. He, himself, on a mission of religious murder was struck blind for a season. It was a temporary judgment, revealing God's mercy. Perhaps this blindness will be short-lived. It is meant for his instruction—not his destruction."

As they moved toward the stairway, Sergius Paulus said, "I have been deeply impressed with the power of Paul."

Neither spoke until they got outside the courtyard. Then John Mark said, "I did not like what happened." Barnabas wondered if he meant the lascivious approach of Elymas or Paul's angry handling of the situation. Mark said nothing else as they walked away.

Back in their room that night, both Mark and Paul were silent. Barnabas wanted to talk. He wanted to hear from them. He longed for conversation about the earthshaking events of the day, but he received no encouragement from either. Barnabas knew how it would feel to be chained between two marble statues in the forum.

Neither responded. Mark sat at a small table and wrote something, while Paul simply stared at a place high on the wall near the ceiling. Barnabas resigned himself to the silence, studying Paul, now mute. Barnabas would have called it sullenness in any other person, but Paul was unlike any other person.

He watched the strangely behaving man and thought how ordinary, how common, was his appearance. Nothing was unusual about his face, which was a reddish tan, almost leathery, like many another farmer's or sailor's because of a refusal to wear any covering in the sunshine. His face, indeed, gave proof that he had been exposed to searing land winds and to broiling winds on the seas. His quick, responsive smile, which revealed a wide separation between his two front teeth, dispelled any aura of greatness. The tension in his life showed itself in his forehead, which had long, graceful curves above his eyebrows and short, stabbling lines just above the bridge of his nose. Paul probably was worn out emotionally from the incantation. He appeared always so quick to denounce any sexual immorality that it seemed he was already armed for the fight or perhaps already at war with the enemy within himself, welcoming a chance to fight the battle outside. The violent Paul had worked a miracle in reverse—not the early wonders of speaking in tongues or gifts of healings, but the hurling of judgment such as the scene that still plagued his own sleep—the upper room and two corpses, friends who had lied to the Holy Spirit. The belligerence of Paul puzzled him.

Barnabas let his eyes move to John Mark and observe the contrast. The young man's teeth seemed too perfect, all fitting close together and radiating brightness. His whole face seemed too handsome to be real, like a classical Greek sculpture. His face reflected the fact that he had enjoyed an easy life, dependent on the sacrifices of an adoring mother. He wondered if John Mark would be scarred by the experience. Yet he knew that every young man . . . His reverie was interrupted by a messenger at the door. Barnabas knew that the runner was not from the governor, because he was dressed in a ragged and haphazard fashion. The Cypriot perceived the scent of salt water and fish in the man's clothing, and he heard him say, "A grain ship leaves tomorrow morning, an hour after sunrise."

The announcement brought Paul to life. He hopped over to the doorway and told the man that he would return with him to the dock to make arrangements for sailing. Without delay, the two left.

"Mark, we should be getting our things ready."

John Mark continued to sit at the table. "Barnabas, I think he's as mad as Herod the Great."

"How can you say such a thing?" He halfway knew what the young man was thinking. This was a holy wrath, my son, but it was not a wild hatred like the great Herod's. He killed for what purpose? Fear of losing power, revenge, and perhaps just plain evil."

"Paul didn't kill, but wasn't his curse just as evil?"

"No, because it was for a purpose. His was a discipline." Barnabas hoped his voice wouldn't tremble and betray his own doubt of Paul's motives. What he wanted to do was present Paul's side, like a counsel for the defense. "He hoped by this means to lead the sinner to the light, much as he came to the light in his Damascus experience."

Barnabas grew worried about Paul's delayed return, and Mark offered to read from his scroll. He read with a melodious voice. It was low and unhurried, almost musical. He read from his own writing, which began with the baptism of Jesus. The Son of Encouragement had heard it many times before.

Paul returned but did not interrupt the reading. With a wave of the hand, he indicated that Mark should continue. At the conclusion, all three remained silent. Then Barnabas asked what Paul had found out. "Everything is ready for the sailing. I went by the palace but was unable to see Sergius Paulus. He was dining, but he sent word that he would come to the dock to say farewell."

Next morning the trio arrived at the waterfront before sunrise. Sailors were winding ropes and loading cargoes. Skins of water were being hauled aboard.

Paul directed his friends to the ship, one of the few that were sailing that time of the year. It was not as large as the enormous grain ships that sailed from Alexandria to Rome. It rode low in the water because it was loaded with copper ore destined for the smelters and coppersmiths of Asia Minor.

After the sun rose over the mountains to the east, Barnabas noticed that the activity around the docks increased. Small boats were putting out to sea for a day of fishing. Repairmen began their work at scraping barnacles or mending sails.

Barnabas and Mark went below to stow their gear. Paul remained on deck to watch for the approach of Sergius Paulus. When they returned to the topside, Paul was still waiting, and the sun was growing warmer. The captain announced that it would soon be time to cast off. Paul became so intent in his watch that he ignored a fly crawling across his cheek.

A messenger from the proconsul arrived and came aboard. Barnabas moved closer to Paul to hear the message. "My master has urgent duties which prevent his coming to say farewell. He wishes you a pleasant voyage and invites your return at any time. He sent you this." He handed him a writing kit, consisting of a wooden framed book of two wax pages and a stylus for writing on the wax. Barnabas knew it was not an expensive gift, and yet it represented something useful to a traveler and scholar. Paul could write notes on the wax pages, and after he had used them, scrape the wax down and write something else. Barnabas could tell that his companion was partially compensated for his disappointment.

A slight breeze was coming in from the ocean, and the captain shouted commands for his ship with its sails still furled to cast off. It headed out of the harbor, propelled by straining and sweating oarsmen below deck. The ship, riding low in the waters, inched out of the boat basin like a clumsy dog paddling. Once it got beyond the northern jetty of the harbor, the captain gave the order for the oarsmen to cease. They or other sailors from below came up, climbed the main mast, and went out on the yardarms to loosen the giant sail in midships. It billowed out in the breeze, and the ship became a graceful dolphin heading northeast, skimming over some of the rollers and through others.

Barnabas was thrilled to be moving. He stood with the other two passengers toward the prow, where an occasional slosh of mist struck them. The wind came from behind, inflating the sail into a graceful arc and moving the boat at maximum speed. Mark wasn't seasick. Paul's delight with his gift soon wore off. He became moody and demanding. "I expect help in the new work."

Barnabas said, "Of course. That's why we came."

"As we get farther from Jerusalem, we will meet fewer Jews. Our work now should be mainly with Gentiles."

John Mark asked, "Do you think the Antioch church had this in mind when they sent you out?" Then he raised another question, a much older one: "If you go to the Gentiles, then will you have to live in their houses and eat with them?"

Paul breathed faster, and his nostrils dilated. He ignored the two questions and turned on the questioner. "You waste time on those scrolls. Writing is what I would like to be doing, but I dare not sacrifice the time." Barnabas knew that Paul told the truth. He was one who loved to study and to write, but he drove himself to talk with people and to teach.

John Mark said simply, "You should make yourself write. If your teachings have any value, they . . ."

Paul was furious. "If, if—did you say if? You are one to say if—you ran away naked from the arrest of Christ."

Barnabas spoke sharply, "Stop, Paul. He was only sixteen."

"What has age to do with . . ."

"You know he was a night watchman in the family garden. He had dropped off to sleep. This lad did the same thing that all the disciples did—he ran away. The only difference was that guards seized his covering. He had to flee in his undergarment." John Mark looked whipped. His chin was touching his chest, and large teardrops fell silently to the deck. "Why did you have to bring up such a humiliating subject, Paul?"

Barnabas had never before heard Paul apologize to anyone. Now Paul confessed, "I have no right to criticize another after the tragic mistakes I made persecuting the church. I am truly sorry."

Appreciative, Barnabas grabbed Paul by the shoulders. Then Paul spoiled his apology. "Yet my life is different now from what it was. That was the old me, not the new me. Now I don't have the same attitudes. God is leading me to something higher." He did not make a verbal contrast—he didn't need to. Both his hearers knew he was implying that John Mark had not changed enough over the years. Paul might as well have said that he thought Mark was still a cowardly adolescent. Things had been said that could not be forgotten.

Three

THREE DAYS LATER when they pulled into the harbor of Attalia, they saw a town rising up from the water like a circular cake with shining white houses and tall green trees on various levels. There was only one ship in the harbor. When they pulled up close to it, sailors shouted greetings back and forth. "We have horses from Cilicia going to Caesarea. We are casting off within twenty-four hours."

One of the Cypriot crew asked, "Can we find a good time in this port?"

"No. There are few people here because of a fever plague. My advice is—go up the river Cestrus eight miles to Perga."

During the steamy trip up the Cestrus river, John Mark spoke quietly, "Cousin, I am going to go on that ship to Caesarea."

It was a spur-of-the-moment decision, not the usual way that he did things, but John Mark decided to leave. He took his scrolls and forgot his other baggage. Barnabas handed him the luggage and hugged him, "God bless you."

Paul said with a kindness that seemed to come too late, "I shall pray for you daily."

Afterwards Paul was talkative, more so than he had been for several days, but now Barnabas felt like retreating, oys-

ter-like, into a shell of silence. He could not listen to Paul
because he felt infected by a sadness that took away his
interest. He grieved for Mark's companionship. He missed
him, and he was worried about his future. The magnificent
sunshine of the humid day served as a contrast to his own
dark feelings. He went below to the cabin, a wounded war-
rior stumbling from a battlefield of bloody casualities and
frenzied horses, exhausted from the combat. Barnabas fell
across his baggage and sobbed. He thought of the sensitive
young man who was now returning to Jerusalem. He wanted
to tell Mark not to feel disgraced when he returned. He
wanted to encourage the young man's talent for collecting
and preserving the stories of Jesus' life.

When the tears on his cheek dried to a salty residue, he
returned to Paul. Now that the younger man had moved off
in another direction, Paul and he were left alone, just as
when they started teaching in Antioch—the two of them
with a common faith and a common work.

Ready to disembark, Paul looked much older than his
forty-eight years. His vision seemed to be getting dimmer.
He still feared recurring fevers, but his sense of mission was
intense. Barnabas said, "Nothing should spoil the understanding of two Christians who have . . . who are on a
mission of giving the good news to a sad world."

The travelers did not tarry in Perga. After only one night,
Paul said, "This humid climate is making my fever return."

"What do you want to do?"

"We must travel on." The apostle rubbed the sleeve of his
robe over his forehead. "Do you think it would be wrong
to leave this place without giving the news here?"

"No," said the Son of Encouragement. "If you remain

here, you would soon be unable to preach. Perhaps we can come back this way. There are many other places that need to hear of the Way."

They began the rugged ascent over the Taurus range. They prayed they wouldn't be stopped by bandits. Finally, the trip became easier. Traveling a well-engineered Roman highway, the missionaries headed for the most important city of the lake region—Pisidian Antioch.

Following their custom, they went directly to the center of the town, where most business and political discussions were bred. At the square of Augustus, they saw a great temple and in front of it a statue with a bull's head. A well-dressed man loitering there watched them and spoke a greeting.

"Are you a citizen of this city?" Paul asked.

"No. The Romans call me 'a dweller,' although my father and grandfather owned property here. But the newcomers from Rome are called 'citizens.' "

Paul lifted his hand toward the stairway and beyond it to the magnificent building. "Isn't this a temple to Zeus?"

"Oh, no. The god with the bull's head, called Men, represents the creative powers of nature. We worship him."

Barnabas said, "I notice he has some competition, with the other temple over there. Is it to the mother-goddess?"

"Yes, we're a people of many religions. All are good."

"Do you know any Jews?"

"Yes, some. I never met a poor one. They are all skilful merchants and moneylenders."

"Where do they live?"

"Near where the city wall overlooks the river Anthius."

They went to the synagogue and met there a teacher

named Baruch. He had hair and beard the color of polished copper; Barnabas recalled a person of similar appearance in the Temple at Jerusalem. He could scarcely keep his mind on the man's words for admiring his ample hair with its dazzling color. Baruch said, "You come to synagogue on the sabbath, and I will call on you to tell about this Messiah. But I warn you—you must have proof. Our people are well trained. I see to that. They will not be cheated in their religion any sooner than they will let a stranger trick them in their money."

At the designated time, they returned to the meeting house with its undecorated stone floor. Before the services they met several Gentiles who were proselytes. After a reading from the law by an aged man who could hardly be heard by the crowd, Baruch read from the prophets. He spoke every sylla- ble distinctly. It was not a mechanical reading, but one with deep feeling. Barnabas thought of Mark's reading.

Barnabas was glad to be called on first. He introduced Paul to them as one who would clarify their searching of the soul and prove the coming of the Messiah from the Scriptures.

Paul spoke a long time, dwelling on a history of the Jewish people and pointing out God's preparation of them to receive his greatest revelation. When he finished, the leader with the copper beard said, "I have listened critically to everything this man has taught from the Scriptures. He has quoted every reference correctly. He knows the law. I want to hear more of his teachings about the Messiah. Let us invite him and his companion to return the next Sabbath, that we can learn more about their belief." People filing out of the synagogue issued their personal invitations to the men to return on the next Sabbath.

It was during their stay in Pisidian Antioch that Barnabas turned forty. It gave him a strange feeling, not justified by any obvious signs, like crossing from one country to another over invisible boundaries. His fortieth birthday caused Barnabas to question his goal. He asked himself what he was accomplishing. He wondered if traveling in the backward provinces of the empire with a fanatical genius—telling about a martyred Galilean—was a sufficient aim. He hadn't hungered for an answer as much since his trip up Mount Carmel. He recalled his previous solution which had really been no answer at all—just a determination to live patiently from day to day. That same patience, he thought, is what I need to relearn.

Several times during the following days they passed by a small temple, and they always noticed a few men leaving or entering. It was a temple to Aphrodite. On one afternoon they saw a large group gathering before it. Unconcerned, Barnabas and Paul planned to skirt the crowd and continue on their way. Something in the atmosphere made them hesitate; it was not the noise of the throng, but rather the lack of it. People, mostly men, gathering in front of the portico, were silent, waiting almost reverently.

The two Christians paused near the rear of the crowd. Soon a priest appeared and gave everyone his blessing. He seemed to be a good-natured, happy man—the kind who would make a success in politics. He talked for a few minutes about the fine weather and hope for good crops. Then he said, "Let the music commence." Two younger men and an older one, dressed in Greek tunics and sandals, ascended the stairs and sat down cross-legged toward the rear of the porch, near the last column to the right. They played their flutes with a clear sound, like the call of a large bird.

Then from the drapery of the temple doorway inched a beautiful young woman. She was fully covered with a thin silk tunic reaching to her ankles. The soft material was drawn tight across her ample breasts. A cord around her waist dropped to the hemline in front. Her lustrous black hair fascinated Barnabas. It was pulled back and tied with a silk hankerchief but fell from the tie into a long cascading appendage like the tail of a fine race horse. Fastened across her forehead in a semicircle was a cluster of shiny gold coins; they lay flat and did not tinkle because her movements were slow and serpentine.

Paul was ready to go, but Barnabas said, "We need to learn what others are thinking."

The girl's style was different from the Arabic dancers whom Barnabas had glanced at through open doorways in Syria. This one was slower, more subtle. Both men looked charmed. Barnabas saw Paul study the movements as the girl threw one long arm forward and then the other. Her whole body swayed to the slow rhythm of the bird-like flutes. Then she began to lift first one foot and the other and glide about the sacred stage. Barnabas saw nothing vulgar about the performance, yet it had a captivating effect on the mostly-male audience.

Now Barnabas was ready to leave; he had seen enough. He did not want to hear the proposition of the priest that would follow. He touched Paul's arm, but he seemed in a trance. He whispered to the apostle, who shook his head. A few minutes earlier he had been the first to want to leave. As the music reached a climax, the sinuous dancer gave a convulsive movement that vibrated her whole frame. The sudden movement snapped Paul back to consciousness, and he sighed, "All right. Let's go."

They moved away in silence. If Barnabas had praised the exhibit, he would have seemed carnal. If he had condemned, he would have felt hypocritical, for he had participated in a few moments of appreciation and thereby had compromised his right to criticize. Paul, who certainly felt the same, said: "Recall the words to a person who has sworn to abstain from wine: 'Take a circuitous route, O Nazarite, but do not approach the vineyard.'" Barnabas had assumed that the apostle had long ago conquered desire, but from his greedy look at the dancer, he knew that it must be a continuing battle for him. Paul said, "Desire is not wrong, but lust is." He explained the difference. "You cannot keep from getting dirt on you as you travel, but you certainly don't have to stop to wallow in a mud bog."

"Right. It's only natural for a person to have some erotic thoughts. Do such things bother you?" Paul's fingers began to fumble with a fold in his robe, and he changed the subject.

They were staying in the home of a man who had been in Jerusalem on the day of Pentecost. Barnabas found in the host a yearning like Mark's for the glorious miracles of the early days. As Paul and the man discussed the meaning of speaking in tongues, Barnabas' mind floated back to the time he was recuperating from his accident. He had watched the girl who was nursing him, Sarah, come into his room, bringing his meals. He recalled the belt around her flowing robe; she seemed to have the smallest waistline in Judea. He had felt a desire—almost uncontrollable—to reach out and pull her to him on the cot.

During the week Paul talked to tentmakers, and Barnabas

talked to potters. They met other proselytes who had not been at the service. They built up a great expectancy about their next preaching service. When the sabbath arrived, the synagogue was filled two hours before the service was to commence. By the time set, the street in front was crowded with people. Suspicious synagogue rulers grew angry, and Baruch told them they simply were jealous.

During Paul's sermon these same leaders interrupted with various remarks and called Jesus by terms that soldiers used to curse their prisoners. Baruch tried to stop the wild shouting of his fellow leaders, but when that feat appeared impossible, he shouted, "Blasphemy." The word was like water thrown on a fire. Then as the crowd grew quiet, they could hear the ripping of his robe, as he expressed his dismay with his fellow Jews.

Paul took advantage of the quietness to announce, "We brought the good news to those who were prepared to receive it, but they have turned it down. So now we turn to the Gentiles." Barnabas on that hot day felt a shiver in his arms as he sensed something final about his friend's pronouncement.

Baruch, with his beard blazing in the sunshine, accompanied them to the central square of the city. There he listened attentively as Paul preached to the Gentiles. The message condemned lust and pronounced judgment on sinners.

"What must we do now?" cried out a man who was weeping.

"Repent, believe in Jesus as Savior, and be baptized."

Baruch said, "Tell them about circumcision." But Paul shook his head.

Barnabas continued the discourse with the red-bearded

believer back at the house of their host. Paul was feeling sick, and Barnabas entertained the rabbi who wanted more information. They talked about the life of Jesus, and the Son of Encouragement made the life as simple as he did to the uneducated converts whom he had catechized in Antioch of Syria. "Every detail fits the Suffering Servant described by Isaiah."

The copper hair nodded in agreement with the story of the Temple cleansing. But Barnabas sensed trouble when he heard the questions spill out. "Did he ever change religions? Did he ever disown his race? Did he ever destroy the Law?"

"No." Barnabas' neck developed an uncomfortable itching.

"Well, then, we should not try to go beyond the Teacher's example. We can be just as scrupulous in the observance of the Law. My father studied with the Pharisees in Jerusalem. I was weaned on the Law. I've spent a lifetime in its study."

"Jesus simplified the Law," added the Cypriot.

"But Jesus never brought a Gentile into the Temple nor ate with one, did he?"

Paul raised his head from his cot, and Barnabas expected a lecture on the way he had confused the new believer. "Tell him to come back. I will discuss God's grace."

Perhaps if Paul had been fully recovered when the copper-colored one returned, he could have convinced him. The fever had subsided, but he was too weak to stand. Barnabas never heard his companion do such a poor job. Finally, Paul dropped to the cot exhausted, and Baruch went to the door. "Brother Paul, you have made me more of a Jew than Moses did."

Next day their hosts rushed in with the news that the high

priest of Aphrodite and the pleasure-loving wife of the Roman tribune had taken out legal papers for the expulsion of Paul and Barnabas from the city. Paul wasn't strong enough to carry his baggage. Thus, Barnabas, laden with luggage and looking like a turtle carrying its house on its back, led his friend toward a safer place. In an ageless ritual, they shook from their robes and their sandals the dust of the inhospitable town. They didn't want to carry even that much of the cruel place with them. After four days of travel, they came to a section of wheat fields and orchards. They enjoyed the last few hours of their journey to the ancient town of Iconium. A native goatherd told them the settlement was so old that it was standing before the flood.

Response to their teaching was amazing. Large segments of Jews and Gentiles believed. Barnabas became fascinated with the idea of growing a beard. It would save him the trouble of shaving. It would identify him with the philosophers of Athens and the holy men of all religions. It could also be thought of as a gesture of defiance toward the Roman custom of shaving. He decided to leave his face to nature.

In two weeks his beard covered his face. In two months, it was full and curly. He had always been plagued by older women saying he had a chubby, baby look. Now strangers in the bazaars showed him courtesy. He developed a new dignity in keeping with his mature look. Students in his class at Iconium gave him a respect that bordered on reverence.

A mistrustful elder of the synagogue sent a young scribe to Pisidian Antioch for some report on their work there. Instead of returning with a message, the scribe brought Baruch back with him.

Thoroughly convinced that he was right and the teachers

were misled, Baruch addressed the synagogue. His eyes glistened, and his lips extended beyond his veiling of copper. He said that he had already sent word of their action to the Sanhedrin in Jerusalem and threatened to follow them to every synagogue they visited.

Conditions grew worse when pagan priests began to find a decrease in temple giving and in sacred prostitution. After several weeks, the visitors addressed a crowd in the forum. When Paul mentioned the word *grace,* the big Jew with beard and hair of copper said, "Expel them." Their former friend might have meant no violence, but the crowd became aroused. People toward the edge of the mob tried to push near. A skinny woman with protruding eyes began to chant: "Leave this town. Leave this town." Everyone took up the cry.

Paul tried to reason with Baruch. No one could hear what he said, but suddenly Barnabas saw the man throw his head back like a rooster ready to crow. The legalist yelled out, "Blasphemy." He tore his cloak in disgust. A forest fire had been ignited by one small bolt of lightning.

Two Roman soldiers pushed into the blaze of angry people and called for order. The crowd felt cheated. The same skinny woman who had begun the chanting started a new theme. "Stone them. Stone them." The mob boiled with rage. But the two tattered teachers had taken advantage of the brief interruption and run outside the town gates.

When they arrived in Lystra, Barnabas felt that they had reached the edge of the world. It was the terminus of the imperial road from Antioch and the last in a chain of fortified Roman towns in that region. But to the fugitives, it was a city of refuge. They were not in town long before they met a child called Timothy. He asked the bearded traveler, "Are you a rabbi?"

Delighted to learn that in that remote place there was at least one Jewish family, they let the boy take them to his home. It was a comfortable house, ruled by the boy's grandmother Lois. The older woman invited the traveling teacher to stay, and the boy led his mother by the hand. She was Eunice, and she stared at their torn clothing.

The grandmother spoke, "You will not find it easy to teach the people of Lystra. They have no background in the prophets. We once lived in Pisidian Antioch, where my daughter met a Roman magistrate." The words about mixed marriage seemed to sizzle on her tongue. "Her husband was transferred here, and I moved to help her when the baby came."

Barnabas said, "Did you know a man in Antioch with a beard the color of copper?"

"Baruch. I have known him since he was a child, long before he was able to grow a beard. He was always lonely. Other children teased him about his hair and called him Fire Head. He refused to play with them. Later his father was killed, and he grew belligerent."

Eunice said, "My husband died from a disease that congested his lungs soon after we moved here. He left us a good home. If we could move it back to Antioch, we would go in a minute."

The older woman said, "I wish we lived in a place where we could send the boy to synagogue school." The Son of Encouragement promised her some help in teaching the child.

Led by young Timothy, Paul and Barnabas went to the bazaar, just inside the gates. In the middle of fruit vendors, cloth salesmen, and beggars, Paul gathered a group of listeners. Someone cackled out, "I want to know my Creator." The voice came from near the ground. Barnabas saw a crippled beggar and noticed Paul moving toward him, like a bee toward a flower. When Paul came so close to the man that their noses were touching, he shouted, "Stand up straight on your feet."

Any spectator who glanced around to see how his neighbors were reacting missed the magic moment. The man who had never taken a step in his life jumped up. The crowd gasped. He walked around. An amazed mob gathered instantly. One of the town elders called several people around him to hear his explanation, and these in turn, spread the story in a widening ripple of gossip. The words *Zeus* and *Hermes* were heard.

Someone led the visitors up to the platform where public addresses were made. Although Paul tried to explain the power of Christ, no one was calm enough to listen except little Timothy. Everybody took part in the excited babble of voices.

Then a blast of trumpets pushed people aside with the force of a dozen elbows. Behind the musicians were girls with flowers and an elderly priest leading two bulls, garlanded with flowers. It was a strange scene, like one enacted on the stage of a theatre.

The religious leader reminded the people of how the gods would frequently leave their sacred home on Mount Olympus to visit mortals. He reminded them that Zeus, the father of the gods, and Hermes, his spokesman, had visited a poor couple not far from that very spot, after being turned away from a thousand doors. Because the old people had welcomed the visitors, they had been rewarded. "Here, again, is Zeus." He pointed to Barnabas, tall and bearded. "And here is Hermes, the messenger." He indicated Paul, short, energetic, and the main speaker. "These same two gods have decided to revisit this beautiful spot. Let us sacrifice these bulls to them with proper ceremony, here and now."

Both men acted on their impulses. Barnabas raised his hands and shouted, "No, No." Paul, steeped in the requirements of law, tore his robe; he seemed to be imitating Baruch's reaction to blasphemy. Each man, noticing the other's reaction, changed; Barnabas tore his garments and Paul shouted.

Instead of remaining on a pedestal, they rushed down to the priest and those surrounding him. They insisted the ceremony be stopped. Then they ran into the crowd, mingling with the people, saying, "We are men of like passions with you."

Their behavior startled the crowd into a loud babble of conversation. Then Paul remounted the platform and preached to them of the Creator's goodness. In his brief message, he pointed to the flowered animals and told the people to turn from such worthless things. The priest was the first to sense that these men were advocates of another religion, men who despised the worship of Zeus. With cheeks puffed in rage, he led the bulls and flower girls back. Others were slower in recognizing the strangers' humanity. They asked questions and touched them and left, chagrined over their gullibility.

The next morning when Paul went to the marketplace, Barnabas felt it his duty to stay with Timothy and give him some promised instruction. He told hero stories of Samson and David; to these he added the heroic adventures of Jesus and of Stephen. When Paul did not return for a midday rest, Barnabas began to grow concerned. Then two of Timothy's young friends came running with news. Barnabas expected trouble. He wasn't prepared for their tidings. "That foreigner got killed," the younger one said.

"People got mad and threw stones at him."

Barnabas felt as if his own blood were draining from him as he listened to the children.

"They dragged him outside the wall and left him there."

Stunned and sickened, Barnabas hoped that the children were mistaken—he feared they had not made up the tale. He had to find out. Grieving would do not good. He must show respect for his friend's battered body, if the story were true, and see to a proper burial before nightfall. Regardless of danger, he would claim the body.

Eunice insisted on going with him. They left Timothy with his grandmother and enlisted two believers to help. When he came near the spot, he saw a limp, bleeding body—discarded on the rocks, attracting flies. Overhead a lone vulture—a scout—circled. As Barnabas knelt to examine Paul's wounds he prayed silently. Then he heard a faint moan from the blood-caked lips. Barnabas touched his companion, and Paul's fingers closed. Barnabas and Eunice praised God. Then Paul pushed himself to a sitting position. He had deep wounds that would leave permanent scars. But he was alive! Eunice helped Barnabas support him back to the house for rest.

A neighbor woman brought a bag filled with lizard skins that she claimed would cure the man if he wore it about his neck. Paul said, "I have a more powerful medicine than your superstitions."

She answered, "You lead a charmed life."

"It's true I've come close to death several times. I escaped from Damascus, later Jerusalem. I have been in mobs that lusted for blood. But the time will come when I will not escape. I am no better than my Master."

The following day Paul felt able to make the trip to a neighboring town, Derbe. In that safer place, he began to preach again the same message that had caused trouble in every town they had visited. Barnabas wished he had Thorn Bush to help him guard Paul from harm.

The months passed and no trouble developed. Then Paul wanted to retrace their steps. He was anxious about the new churches. They went back and led in the election of elders in each congregation. In almost every place, the believers said that they wanted both apostles—they were now classing Barnabas in that group despite his objection—to return to Antioch and give their appreciation to the Christians who had sent out these missionaries.

On the return voyage, Paul looked exhausted. "Barnabas, I wish I had some physician to travel with me." He hadn't said "with us."

Back in Antioch, Lydia was buying vegetables near the gate. She didn't recognize Barnabas because of his beard. When Thorn Bush saw it at the basilica that night, he was delighted. It gave him the nickname he wanted. For at least a week, everyone called the Cypriot the Goat. Antioch was more like home than Cyprus. He had allowed the ropes of friendship to rot. All he had in Cyprus was a puzzled mother. He said to Thorn Bush, "I'm glad to be home."

Back in their room after the service, Barnabas said, "When

you tell about our trip again, I wish you would make two changes. Leave out the conversion of the proconsul of Cyprus, but add the story of how you faced the stoning mob at Lystra." Paul grunted.

Thorn Bush came by the inn to tell them that he was leaving for Alexandria with a load of parchment. He admitted that his real purpose was to look for Rhoda.

The days were golden ones, filled to the brim with enjoyment. Every meal brought an invitation to a different home—Titus, Manaen, Lydia, and many others. All this continued when Peter came from Jerusalem. He had come to check on some questions about their teachings. He joined in the round of entertainment.

Suddenly the parties stopped. Frowning men, claiming to be sent from James, reprimanded Peter for eating with defiled people. They explained that the pure faith was in danger of dilution. The laws of Moses, they explained, must be respected.

Barnabas could sympathize with Peter. Like himself, the fisherman had always shrunk from public ridicule. He wanted to be everyone's friend. He accepted the delegation's criticism, not completely understanding it and not agreeing with it, yet seeking to hold on to their favor. Peter visited in no more Gentile homes and abstained from eating at the services when there was a non-Jew at the table.

Barnabas reasoned that if the co-head of the church set such an example, he should also follow it. Paul, however, flaunted his freedom in their faces. He ate with anyone who invited him. Then he called for a mass meeting of all believers in Antioch, making sure the men from Jerusalem would be present.

His speech was unforgetable. He said, "I hate to criticize anyone. But when a person is wrong, he is wrong. I had rather say something in a meeting like this than to his back. Thus I want to charge Peter with playacting, hypocrisy, with taking a role which is not his real character."

Even though hundreds of people were present, no one coughed. Every ear was straining to hear the charge. "The Lord led him to the house of one of the first Gentile converts, after giving him a glorious vision. Now he has turned his back on this truth and refuses to eat with followers of Christ who have not been circumcised." He pointed his finger at the apostle. "Peter, you are wrong, and you know it. You have led even Barnabas away from the truth."

A lightning bolt of fact shook the frame of the Cypriot. To hear his name defamed in a public gathering was a shock. Lydia leaned over to put a plump hand on his shoulder and said, "Tell them it's not true." He said nothing, but waited for Peter to reply. The apostle looked as if he had heard a cock crowing once again.

Some of Antioch's leaders stood up, fumbling for words, and began questioning the committee from James. The visitors suggested a solution. The whole matter should be submitted to the apostles and mother church in Jerusalem for a decision.

The trip south took them again to Caesarea, where they learned from Philip's daughters that Cornelius was providing for services in his home. "Does he have room enough for the large group?"

"Yes, his is one of the finest homes in Caesarea. It was formerly called the House of the Laughing Satyr."

The Son of Encouragement felt his mouth drop open. "I

thought it was owned by a widow."

"Not any more. She was killed by a jealous lover in a drunken quarrel. She had no heirs, and the centurion Cornelius was able to secure the place from the city officials."

In a stupor he said, "I would like to go there again."

The polished gate looked exactly the same, but the atrium was different. Instead of the happy statue, surrounded by shrubbery, there were only flagstones paving the added space for church attenders. Barnabas asked the host, "What happened to the sculpture that gave the house its name?"

"I don't have a household of slaves, as the former owner did. So when we were preparing the courtyard as a meeting place, I asked some of the believers to help with the work. They commented on how ugly and sensuous it was. As they were carrying it to the back, it dropped to the paving and broke. Would you like to see what is left?" Cornelius escorted the Cypriot to a little storage room at the rear of the house, littered with pieces of pottery. He saw the laughing satyr with arms and head knocked off. He wondered how anyone could be blind enough to call him ugly or careless enough to drop him. Yet Barnabas consoled himself with the fact that he would soon see a lad in Jerusalem whose arms were not made of marble.

When they reached Jerusalem, he found Sarah, patient and serene, wearing a faded blue dress. He realized it was the same one she was wearing the last time he saw her. He wondered if they were living off charity until he saw the other occupant of the house. Jacob was wearing a Roman tunic, white with an embroidered border. Barnabas still thought of him as *the boy,* although Jacob was shaving now. The Son of Encouragement could think of only one word to describe his appearance: skinny. Gone was the beauty of childhood. He was a gawky youth. Barnabas looked with sympathy on the long, thin neck with a knot protruding at the front. "Welcome, Barnabas." He pitched his voice lower than a natural sound.

Barnabas hugged him but felt no responding embrace. "We have much to talk about."

"Can't. I'm going to the hippodrome." The word, which sounded natural in Caesarea, sounded out of place in Jerusalem. "All the young men go—except some from strict families and the Christians."

Sarah said, "He told me he found some money there. He brought home a bag full."

Barnabas felt he was with a stranger he wanted to get to know. The boy had been like his son. As with Rufus, he knew he couldn't unravel months of spinning with one tug, so he changed the subject: "Have lamps been selling well?"

"Yes, very well. And I have been experimenting with a new type. It is made in a mold and not on a wheel. It can be produced much faster. Sarah will show you one."

He slammed the door, and she sighed, "Do you want to see it?"

He nodded and wondered about her reluctance. In the pottery shop that had once belonged to Zadok, he looked at the molded lamp and understood. The lamp, similar to her grandfather's Herodian lamps in size, had a much smaller filling hole in the middle and more room on the top for decoration. The design around the border of the reservoir led his eyes to the figure. It looked like Zeus surrounded by stars. "What do you think of it?" she said slowly.

"I was thinking of Zadok. He spent his entire lifetime

making one simple, unadorned lamp after the other. He treasured the pattern that had been handed down to him, which he hoped to pass . . ."

"He would not rest easy if he knew."

"Sarah, what has happened to the boy?"

"I wasn't equal to it." She began to sob and fell into his arms. "It is good that the Lord never gave me children of my own. I have failed with Jacob."

"I am not blaming you. I am more to blame. I should have been here to help him as a father would."

"Jacob has changed." She touched the tip of her sleeve to her moist eyelids. "He never attends services anymore. He says he had enough religion as a child and is now tired of it. He doesn't talk much, but once he said he wanted to enjoy life as the Romans do."

That night Barnabas attended the conference. Many people were present to hear the two travelers relate their experiences in the Gentile world. Yet at the conclusion, a group of Pharisees who had accepted Christ came before the group. Barnabas was amazed to recognize a man with hair and beard the color of copper. Baruch had come to the Holy City. He spoke. "These men brought the story of the Messiah to many Gentiles in my area." He waved his arm toward Barnabas and Paul. "Someone must go back to these same people. They have been led halfway out of the wilderness. Some authority must go back and compel them to be circumcised. They must keep the law of Moses."

Back at the potter's house, Barnabas could not have slept if he had been drowsy. The outcome of the meeting had been disappointing. The opposition had been strong, and the missionaries had not presented their case as well as they had hoped. Further, he wanted to stay awake and have a talk with the boy when he came in. The youth did not return during the night.

The next day, sleepy Barnabas had to appear before James and the elders for a conference that was called a private investigation. After it was over, he returned to the house and saw a cart in the doorway. Two large men were loading Zadok's pottery wheel onto the wagon.

"What are you doing?" Barnabas demanded. He charged up to them, as he had often done in the wrestling ring.

"Taking what is lawfully ours."

"What proof do you have?"

"We handed proof to this woman."

Then Barnabas noticed Sarah slumped against the doorpost, holding a piece of pottery with a receipt written on it. She looked so pitiful that he said nothing. As the worker set the wheel in place, he said: "The boy wanted money to apply to his passage to Rome. It wasn't easy for us to find that much. He must be halfway to Caesarea by now."

Barnabas knew he must hold up for Sarah's sake. He could not let himself break down. He said, "God help us."

She ran to get a comb, and then began to laugh hysterically as she combed her hair. The laughter was louder than the racket of the cart moving away, filled with merchandise made from the dreams of a lifetime. Barnabas wanted Sarah to cry. He could stand weeping better than high-pitched giggling. Gaily she asked, "Are you ready to eat?"

He sat at the table and she placed a lighted lamp before him. She busied herself cooking the evening meal, but he just sat there staring at the flame. The light, burning steadily from a lamp made by the old man with the chewing lips, illuminated his grief. Barnabas prayed, *Lord, why can I never hold on to one I love? Help me bear the loss of another one.* When Sarah went out to get some cheese from a neighbor, he sobbed until his shoulders were sore from shaking. *I had rather the high priest had taken him,* he said to himself. *I saved him from bullies to lose him in this way. I lost the others to death—except for Rufus. I think death was easier. This is different.* He whispered aloud, "If he had died a martyr, I could have borne it better."

He spent a long time calling the roll of his departed loves: his wife, the rabbi, Zadok, Stephen, and even Ananias and Sapphira. He might have spent the whole night in moody contemplation, but Sarah put before him a steaming soup that he tried to eat. The meal was tasteless. The conversation was almost an argument, with each trying to take the blame. Barnabas said: "I spent too much time with other people. I took his faith for granted. I should have stayed here with him."

"Perhaps he was jealous of the attention you gave me." She blushed.

"You were not to blame." He knew he had given her even less attention than the lad. "My fault."

"No, Joseph, you did everything—more than an earthly father. You were a spiritual father to him." When she said these words, her false gaiety broke down, and she threw herself across the table. Barnabas, brokenhearted, was relieved. He placed his hand on her trembling shoulder and felt her wrestling with her grief.

Four

THE NIGHT FOR the appointed meeting arrived. The Jerusalem Conference had to decide. Before the meeting, everyone was polite but strained. Few people chatted. New arrivals spoke a brief word of greeting and took their places. One disciple stood to speak. Although his voice was accustomed to speaking to large groups, it was thin and quavery. He stumbled over some words. He usually preached with many gesticulations, but now he held both of his useless hands before his stomach in an awkward way, with fingertips touching.

Another read from a scroll. His hands shook so badly that he had to stop and try to get control of the trembling pointer he held. Baruch had a confident smirk on his fat lips, glistening between the layers of red brightness. Members seemed frightened. There was no physical danger; however, someone behind Barnabas whispered, "This could change the message as we know it."

When it came time for Barnabas to speak, he tried to express what was on his heart but couldn't concentrate on the meeting. His mind was on a ship, perhaps even at that moment, taking on passengers for Rome. He sat down dejected.

Baruch was furious, and his speech was disconnected.

Then Paul spoke. His words were well chosen and his ideas clear. "At a common meal believers find the deepest expression of Christian fellowship. If they are divided there, then there is no real unity." He stared at Barnabas as he said those words. Then he introduced Titus, who made the shortest but most effective talk of the evening.

Finally, when eyes were droopy and lamps were going out, a sandy-haired believer named Silas, looking a lot like Thorn Bush, made a suggestion that each side forfeit a little ground. On that neutral territory could be built a compromise. The heads that were not nodding from sleep nodded in agreement.

James stood and stated the terms of the compromise. "It is my judgment that we do not require circumcision of the Gentiles, but that we order them to abstain from unclean food and unclean living." The high priest himself could not have sounded any more authoritarian.

Everyone but Baruch, however, seemed satisfied. From the flaming beard came the announcement that he was leaving for Joppa immediately. The congregation agreed to come back together to approve the written form and to appoint two messengers to accompany the missionaries back to Antioch. They chose the one who had made the compromise suggestion, Silas, and a man from one of the first families of the church, Judas bar Sabbas. The group headed for Antioch, where they hoped the decision would be joyfully received.

Homecoming was again joyous. The trip to Jerusalem had not kept Barnabas and Paul away from Antioch as long as the missionary trip, but the young men who loved nicknames called them snails for taking such a long time in returning. His old friend Thorn Bush invited Barnabas to move into his house on the day of their return and told him that a surprise awaited him at the service that night. Later, that same day, Manaen invited the visitors to lodge in his home. Barnabas, afraid of offending the leatherworker's hospitality, remained in the simple house outside the walls, while Paul moved into the ornate house of Manaen—silent about its classic beauty.

Judas and Silas stayed with Titus, when they were not traveling to various nearby congregations to deliver the decree in person.

As Barnabas walked into a basilica full of well-wishers, one head stood out. Copper hair that seemed to have a higher polish than even Baruch's drew him. He left other embraces and hugs to get to Rhoda. She appeared to be only a few months older than young Jacob as he enfolded her in his arms. Thorn Bush beamed, "This is our surprise for you." Barnabas called it the best gift possible and learned that the slave girl had returned with Thorn Bush to her owner and begged forgiveness. Her mistress forgave, demanded no punishment, and promised she would attend one of the Christian services.

When Paul was not troubled with high temperatures and bad eyesight, he joined his companion in teaching the maturing Christians of Antioch. Their work appeared harmonious, but Barnabas realized that something was festering like a boil that had to come to a head. He was not surprised at what happened at a service one night. He regretted that Rhoda's mistress was present on that occasion.

As soon as three stars could be seen, the sabbath was over

and the Lord's Day began. Barnabas and Paul attended the meeting in the house of Benjamin Ben Ezra, a jewel merchant and skilled craftsman who could engrave scarabs and carve cameos. Rhoda's mistress knew him. This frugal man had accumulated a sizeable amount of wealth, and his new house was one of the largest in the Jewish section, surpassing that of Manaen. Early arrivers sat on stone benches against the inside walls. He saw Paul among this group. Other wooden chairs and benches had been brought in for latecomers. Some of the adolescents sat around the edge of the central pool, the *impluvium,* under the opening in the tile roof. A youth touched the water surface and flipped a few drops toward his older friend Titus.

The meal before the service was more like a picnic than a banquet. The crowd was too large to allow for the customary reclining about tables, banquet style. Each person simply sat in a chair or on a bench and balanced his plate. People had brought boiled eggs, dried figs, salted fish, olives, bread, and dates. These had been spread on a table near the center of the courtyard.

The pastor, an older man who had been elected to act as the president and guide of the congregation, prayed aloud and then lighted the candles on the table. All came by the table to select food. Each person took a moderate amount. The wealthy host who provided the wine, walked among the busy eaters and filled their cups. Ever so often Barnabas glanced across at Paul, who looked withdrawn.

The next part of the service was the breaking of bread. After the group sang a psalm, the pastor read from Isaiah in the popular Greek translation. Then he repeated the words of the institution. He had been instructed by Simon Niger, who had arrived from Jerusalem six years earlier.

When the pastor asked for requests for prayer, someone mentioned an absent widow who was ill. A young girl asked about taking the elements of the Supper to her. Paul quickly vetoed the idea. Someone else asked prayer for a believer whose husband was a prisoner in Jerusalem.

After the prayer, the pastor asked, "Does anyone have a *charisma,* a gift, to share?" Three men declared they had the gift of interpreting certain Old Testament scriptures on the Messiah and demonstrated it. Then the sixteen-year-old granddaughter who had requested prayer said she had no real gift but would like to share a song she had written.

Simon of Cyrene repeated the story of Jesus' death and resurrection. The audience was deeply moved. The speaker stood in his place, exhausted from the emotional ordeal of remembering the exact words. The service was dismissed, but no one was ready to leave. People stood talking with one another, and several clustered around Simon. John Mark asked him several questions.

Barnabas drifted toward Paul, who was talking with the young singer, vigorously shaking his head in her face. He heard the girl say, ". . . can see no reason for denying the Supper elements to my grandmother."

"I am an apostle, called by the living Christ. He has given me directions." The girl gave a casual shrug, lifting her shoulders, and started away. Barnabas spoke to her briefly, telling her what a blessing her song had been.

Paul frowned. "Why were you so kind to her, after you heard the way she questioned my authority?" Rhoda's mistress heard.

"She is a girl with great possibilities for the church. She

needs to be encouraged."

"Barnabas, you are always willing to see the good in someone before the person is tested."

"You forget, Paul." Barnabas heard a group singing a psalm over in a corner. "I was willing to bet on you when no one else would." Barnabas thought of how a breaker of sea foam dashes against a rock, covering it for a moment with bursting and melting froth, but making no lasting impression on the hard surface. "Paul, we must talk."

The answer was curt. "We are talking now."

"I mean . . ." The noise of the fellowship grew louder. "Let's go back, to the peristyle." In the rear court were two small lanterns, giving just enough light to keep a person from falling into the black oleander bushes. Barnabas began slowly, "I have been thinking of our work together in Cyprus and Galatia.

Before he could continue, Paul responded, "I have been concerned, too. I would love to see our early converts. I am uneasy about them. I am afraid of false teachers like Baruch."

Barnabas attempted to talk of their relationship, which at the moment seemed as open and cordial as it had ever been. "You have a distinct gift for working with Gentiles."

Without disputing the truth of the statement, Paul said, "My calling. I must use it in the right way. I would like to check on Sergius Paulus. I am sure he needs my tutelage."

Barnabas tried again. "I have lost something. I want to regain it."

Paul was lost in his own forest of ideas. "We must return to our labors. Every farmer knows that he can't plant seeds and forget about them. They must be fertilized and watched after."

"That is true. The work is going well here. Nothing should stop us from going. John Mark is able to travel. He could . . ."

Paul declared, "Not John Mark."

"But, Paul, you know he was a great help to us when we started out. Remember how he helped us unload at Cyprus. He was thrilled to be a part of the work. Certainly, he will have the same enthusiasm again."

"Possibly, but that enthusiasm will burn out just like those flickering flames in the lamp holder yonder. Then all will be dark. Yes, he might start out ablaze, but he would burn out."

"Paul, he needs to get away from his manuscripts. He needs to be in active work. Have faith in him, Paul."

"I have faith. I also have hope and love." Paul's mind became distracted with three words he had used, and he repeated them, "Faith, hope, love."

"Surely you will give him another chance."

Paul moved toward the archway to the atrium. "Never. I am ready to go with you alone whenever you can get ready." He left the semi-darkness and returned to the group in the front court. Barnabas watched the apostle's cloak spread behind him like a falcon's wings spread back for a plunge earthward.

Barnabas lingered in the gloom of the garden court. He felt reprimanded and rejected. It was as if he had taken some impossible request to Claudius Caesar, such as building a Christian temple in Rome. The Emperor's negation would be final. No senate, no court of appeal would alter it. *But wait,* he said to himself, as the fresh breeze of a new idea blew over him, *there is an appellate court here, the church itself.*

He knew that the church that set them apart in the first place would make any decision for another commissioned trip.

Back in the atrium, almost all the congregation was still present. Torches on the wall were putting forth illumination and giving the courtyard the pungent smell of burned oil. Paul was talking with the pastor. Barnabas interrupted them. "Paul, since we can't reach a decision on this matter of another trip, why not seek the advice of the church?" The man from Tarsus squinted in unbelief. "The church, which sent us out the first time, can decide who will be sent out on another trip."

"My decision has been made." Paul's voice was higher pitched than usual, and the pastor sensed a serious rupture.

"Brothers," the leader said, "if there is any disagreement, let us not unsettle the church."

The Son of Encouragement reassured him. "We will do nothing to harm the church. I would willingly go to the cross for this church. But the congregation can break our deadlock in thinking. We seek their advice."

"I, Saul of Tarsus, do not seek it. The Lord Christ has spoken to me." He used his old name, and the fires of zealotry burned in his eyes.

Barnabas looked at the worried pastor and spoke. "I still want the spiritual counsel of the congregation." Rhoda, her mistress, and Lydia walked over to see what the discussion was about. Others joined them in a large circle. Barnabas folded his arms and looked square into the face of the congregational leader. Paul was trying to say something, but Barnabas continued. "God has spoken through this group before. He can do it again. Paul knows this. He hasn't had time to pray about this new idea. When he does, he will follow the congregation." He felt he had concluded, but he knew he had omitted something that honor demanded him to say, "And if the church decides against Mark, I shall abide by the decision."

"Very well, if you think best," said the pastor. And he began to clap his hands to attract the attention of the others. "We shall come together tomorrow night at the basilica of law for a very important meeting. It concerns another trip by some of our beloved brethren. Leave tonight in the spirit of prayer. In your work tomorrow, continue in prayer, and come tomorrow night seeking the Lord Christ's leadership in this important matter."

When Barnabas entered the lighted basilica, he saw a large crowd of people. Thorn Bush, sandyheaded and conspicuous, was talking with the pastor. The bushy head bobbled up and down as he talked. The sick widow who had been absent the night before was there on a stretcher. Two men who had begun to lose interest in the custom of the Supper were present. When Barnabas spotted John Mark, he called him aside.

The younger man said, "There are many people here tonight, more than I expected." *Especially one,* Barnabas thought, wondering why no one had made clear to Mark that he was not to attend. *If there is a battle, I hope there will be no casualties.*

"You should not be present for this. It will do you no good."

"I know. You don't want me to see Paul reveal himself as he really is."

Barnabas wanted to be truthful, but he didn't want to discourage the young man. As Mark turned away, Barnabas added, "I will tell you about it."

Before Barnabas had time to exhale his worry over Mark, Thorn Bush came up to him and said: "I've had a successful week, and I want to make a contribution. Apply this to your trip." He pressed into his hands some gold pieces decorated with the Emperor's portrait.

"The trip isn't definite yet."

Someone else heard about the money idea and pushed a silver coin into his hand. Barnabas tried to give it back, but the person had moved into the crowd. Several others went back to the door and dropped coins into an empty bowl there.

"What are they doing?" It was Paul's voice.

Barnabas waited for Thorn Bush to explain, but there was silence. "Paul, some of them wanted to give some money toward the expenses of our trip."

"Who told them of my need for money?" Paul squinted.

Everyone in the large assembly room grew quiet, listening to their teachers. "I didn't ask for it. These people wanted . . ."

"You should *not* have accepted it without my permission. Before I go on a trip, I must spend time in prayer. I need to know what God wishes."

Barnabas began to plead, using the same tone he had often used with the boy in Jerusalem. "God wishes us to go on a trip. Surely, this money is a symbol of his favor. I feel sure . . ."

Paul interrupted, "How can you know the will of God?"

Barnabas spoke very slowly. "The same way you can, Paul. Don't you think I can? Do you think you are the only vessel God can . . ."

"I believe that God works through other people," he admitted. To Barnabas it seemed as if Paul were trying to cover himself with a mantle of prophetic aura. The Cypriot resisted. Yet he knew, as well as he knew the coastline of Cyprus, that Paul was sincere. Paul walked to the front of the basilica where charges and countercharges were made in legal cases daily. Barnabas, following him to the front, heard him mutter, "I still don't approve of your receiving a collection without consulting me."

The meeting did not take long. Barnabas was glad his cousin had gone because Paul said some bitter things about the young man's defection. The words were all true, but Barnabas tried to defend the young man's actions. The surprise of the evening came when the arguments were interrupted by Thorn Bush. "Barnabas believes in giving a person a chance to overcome failure. Very well, let him take John Mark and go to Cyprus, his homeland." The suggestion sounded reasonable, yet it seemed a rebuke to leave Paul behind. Titus stood to speak, but the leather merchant continued. "Let Paul go to his homeland, Tarsus, and beyond. Let him take with him Silas or someone else he trusts. We can divide money between the two and pray for both."

The pastor jumped to his feet before anyone had a chance to object and declared, "The Lord has spoken through this brother. Praise the Lord. This church can serve him better with two groups going out than with just one. All who favor this plan, stand and raise your arms in prayer."

Although he prayed a long prayer, people continued to hold up their arms. Barnabas held his palms outstretched, as if he were trying to catch something falling. He prayed that Silas would be patient with his traveling companion.

Five

THORN BUSH WENT with Barnabas and his cousin to the seaport. He would be sailing, too, but in a different direction, toward Caesarea or Joppa. "I will work a while in Jerusalem."

"It's not a safe place," Mark said.

"I know, but I'm not afraid."

"Thorn Bush, I want you to look after someone who is very dear to me." Barnabas' throat clogged up. "Like a sister." He told her name and where to find Sarah.

The leatherman walked on down the wharf to inquire about other vessels, and the cousins stood before their ship, the *Aphrodite,* in the last stages of loading, looking like a bird preening her feathers before a flight homeward.

Barnabas' eyes darted over the wharf and its workers, not finding the face they sought. He knew that Paul was there in Seleucia, visiting the congregation of Titus, and he yearned for a final conversation with his brother in Christ. "Go on board, Mark. Find a safe place for your manuscripts. I will join you in a minute."

He watched the last skins of water being taken aboard the ship named for the goddess of love. Then he heard the captain command the sailors to take their stations. Suddenly, he spied Paul. "My brother, you have come."

"You are alone, I see. Has the quitter deserted you already?"

Like a cake spoiled before it is ever placed in the oven, the meeting was already a failure. Barnabas could not find words to express his disappointment. "You've hurt me."

He looked at a different man from the one he had seen on a dock at Tarsus. The smile was gone. A large scar tissue, received from the stoning at Lystra, circled over his forehead like a pink worm.

"You have no cause to feel hurt."

"You know, Paul, that you were wrong to speak out in the meeting as you did."

"No, I was right. If I had it to do over, I would do the same." His nostrils dilated and contracted as he breathed.

"Please, Paul, keep your voice down. Someone might hear."

"I don't care if they do. I would stand before God's throne and say the same thing. I know that John Mark is a quitter and will never be any account for the work."

"There is a difference in us, Paul. I am man enough to admit it when I'm wrong. But I seldom heard you say you were mistaken. I believe you are too stubborn to do it."

In a rage, Paul answered, "I resent being called stubborn. I did what is right, and I shall continue to do what is right. God will show me."

"Yes, my friend, but how can you be sure that God is leading you?" Barnabas asked the question calmly, with sincerity.

Paul's face became flexible and reddish. The veins on his forehead glowed a dark blue; others in his neck throbbed.

"I am afraid this conversation is wasting time for both of us."

Above the noise of the pier workers, the captain's voice sang out to the crew to loose the moorings and head for the open waters. Paul looked around and prepared to leave. Barnabas wondered if it would end like this. His heart was sinking with grief. He put his hand on Paul's shoulder, not daring to look at him, and said hoarsely, "I will be praying for you."

He went up the gangplank just before it was removed. He was leaving a portion of his life on the wharf. He had given the man a devotion surpassed only by that to Christ. He had offered his loyalty to this man who had just called their conversation a waste of time. He had loved him with a dedication that others reserve for wife and children. He had spent some of the most hallowed times of his life in the presence of the man with bulging veins and ugly scars.

Their relationship had been extinguished. The wick and the lamp had been separated. Only the cold, unilluminated object remained. Gone—irreparably gone, was the warm, glowing companionship of former years. There was no spark, no incandescence, no miracle of light, only smoldering memories.

Seamen cast off the moorings. From the moving deck, he looked back for a last glimpse of Paul. The man from Tarsus saw that Mark stood by Barnabas. The apostle's face was drained of its rudiness and now looked as gray as a raincloud. He smiled. From across the water, he made a strange gesture. He pointed to himself, and next he held up his hands toward the sky. Then he pointed to the man from Cyprus and the young man from Jerusalem. Barnabas understood. He was saying he would pray for both of them. A fourth gesture, unplanned, followed. Paul wiped his eye on the sleeve of his cloak.

Barnabas waved and watched the quay until the apostle's face became as small as the jot of a Hebrew scribe. Then he realized the separation was final. Barnabas doubted that he would ever again see the tentmaker from Tarsus. Their missionary journeys were now only an evaporating memory. The separation seemed as final as death.

He began to feel saturated with sadness. When one pulls away from his closest companion, he leaves a vacant spot, like the removal of a nail from wood. Barnabas understood the melancholy, and it was bearable, but tears formed in his eyes. He remembered dangers of their work in Pisidian Antioch and in Lystra and successes in the happy street called Jawbone. His cheeks were drenched with the bittersweet waters of memory.

His cousin made no inquiry, but was ready with a cheerful word when Barnabas seemed ready to talk. They discussed the dangers of the mission and the importance of the work.

Salamis looked just as it had the day he left it. His mother was overjoyed to see her son and nephew, but worried over their safety. When they talked about the Messiah, she listened. When Mark explained about his mother, she said, "My sister believes this?" They stayed with a friend west of the city. Brave people attended the services. A time came when the work reached a level of self-guidance. Barnabas and Mark left, visiting many places they had been before, but avoiding Paphos. The work in Cyprus was about like work everywhere else—slow and deliberate. Except for the sudden spurt of growth when he first went to Antioch, Barnabas had not seen any great successes. He found that most congregations required months of cultivation before a modest harvest could be expected. He continued to look for the exception, the miracle, but it never happened.

On the day they finally went into Paphos, they learned that the proconsul was building a temple to honor the Emperor. Although Barnabas was not overwhelmed by surprise, he was deeply concerned by the gesture and what it might mean to the safety of Christians on the island. He was not prepared to hear, just at that moment, John Mark's statement: "I want to return to Jerusalem."

"You would do this again?"

"My mother is getting old, and I want to check on her. I also want to compare some manuscript details with Peter."

"Go at any time."

Mark paused. "No. I will not desert you. I would like to leave within a year, but I want you to have time to replace me."

Barnabas, relieved that his cousin was not thinking of an immediate desertion, began to think of a replacement. He decided he would look for a substitute in Alexandria, where he had heard of an excellent training school for church leaders. Perhaps he could find someone and return within a few months.

Because of a fever he contracted on the trip to Egypt, the events were more like a dream than reality. He found some old friends from Jerusalem in the Alexandria congregation and made some new ones. People there still talked of Rhoda, and they had heard she was married. Barnabas found no new worker who had the qualities of a Paul or even a Mark. He felt weakened by the sickness and disappointed by the fruitless search. The trip would have been a complete failure, except for the discovery he made on his return voyage. On the grain ship which was to stop in Caesarea, he found his early travel companion, Julius of the Augustan cohort. They talked of old times and of the new faith.

"I have accepted Christ as my Lord, even though it will probably mean no more advancements for me in the military."

"Do you know Cornelius?"

"Yes, I attend services at his place, the House of the Laughing Satyr."

"I have been there, too." If he had felt stronger, he might have explained what he knew of the statue that gave the house its name. He preferred to let the laughing boy rest in his dusty mausoleum.

"We are about to outgrow it, but we don't know what to do. The authorities will not let us use any of the public buildings. They are afraid of offending the Emperor."

"Tell me about Cornelius. Is he in your same unit?"

"No, there are five cohorts in Caesarea. He belongs to the Italian cohort. His troops respect him, even the ones who have rejected the Way."

Barnabas did not get to see Cornelius. The closer the ship sailed to Caesarea, the more his head ached. As much as he wanted to see his friends there, he asked Julius not to tell anyone that he was on board the ship in the harbor.

The days sailed past, as the ship glided toward his island home. The fevers and headaches lessened. As he stood, wobbly, at the prow and watched the harbor of Salamis on the horizon, he thought of the simple words, my homeland. They were a prayer of thanksgiving.

On his return to Cyprus, Barnabas dismissed Mark. Alone

in the little farmhouse, now deserted, on the western edge of Salamis, he pondered his cousin's leaving. Sadness seemed to be a regular part of his diet. My life is nourished by good-bys, he said to the echoing walls.

When he went to the congregation, a spokesman informed him, "We don't require your teaching any longer. You are free to leave us and travel about the island." Perhaps it was meant as a generous gesture, but it came at the wrong time. Just when he wanted to lose himself in a busy schedule of teaching and preaching, he found that he was not needed. He felt disarmed and vulnerable. Like a becalmed ship, he existed, waiting, from hour to hour.

He began to travel, but he took sadness with him like a piece of luggage. The loneliness he once lost in the house of the potter returned. The troubles of travel, which he had shared with Mark, were now bottled up inside himself. The dangers, which Paul's companionship had once minimized, now seemed to grow each day. Jews were in disfavor with the government; Christians were in danger.

After his cough grew worse, he returned to the little deserted farm house at Salamis. He found things in the city in an uproar. He learned much from his mother. Although she was not a professing Christian, she knew what was happening among the followers of the Way. "Their leader has been jailed," she said.

"Do you mean the one who told me I was not needed?"

"Yes. He refused to burn incense to Caesar. After his arrest, he appealed to Caesar and was sent to Rome."

"Surely he will be released."

"My son, what will you do when they ask you to burn incense?"

"I will refuse."

"You could burn it, Joseph, without saying Caesar is Lord. You could save your life without blaspheming." Her eyes darted about the room, avoiding his.

"Never."

"I knew you would say that." She ran her hand over a smooth piece of material that was waiting for delivery. "Your father would be proud of you."

"What of yourself?"

"I doubt that I will ever be tried publicly. I am not important enough. But if they asked me, I would refuse, too."

"Mama, have you accepted Jesus as the Messiah?"

"I am too confused to know." She moved her hands as if she were wringing out a wet garment. "I simply cast myself on God's mercy." She walked to the door and scouted the way. "Come back tomorrow afternoon, and we will talk more of the Messiah."

Word arrived during the night from Mark that his own mother was dying in Jerusalem and was asking for her sister. The matriarch left her empire of caldrons and dye samples, determined to go to her sister and resigned to spending her own last days in the Holy City.

Some months later John Mark arrived in Cyprus. He told of his mother's death. The Cypriot sister had arrived in time to nurse her during the final days. He reported that Rhoda had been set free by her mistress who was now a believer. Rhoda and Thorn Bush had gotten married. No one had heard from Jacob.

John Mark was ready to return to work. Barnabas was overjoyed to have him but concerned about a cough and weakness. "Has my mother accepted the Messiah?"

"She has never said."

"She's a stubborn one."

"She attends the meetings, saying they could do her no harm."

With the believers in Salamis growing careless and discouraged, Barnabas decided to concentrate on the situation there. He reentered the work of teaching and evangelism with all his strength, as if it were the final round in a wrestling match. He seemed to draw energy from the waning days of summer and from his cousin. The man whom Peter had named the Son of Encouragement discovered that he had to receive encouragement before he could dispense it. He began a new habit of rising early to pray, and he wished that he had started it as a younger man.

One day Mark, with lines in his brows, came from the city. "This place is as dangerous as any city in the empire."

"Why is it?"

"Money. Local people are not making the money they once did. They're resentful."

"Perhaps they are worried over the delay of the rainy season." Barnabas recalled another rainy season that had been delayed and then arrived late like an invading army.

"No, it is money. Not many people are visiting the temple prostitutes. The silversmiths and goldsmiths are not selling as many figurines as they formerly did."

"Mark, we're succeeding. The Lord is changing the city." He tried not to cough.

"They're blaming this spirit of reform on us. Of course, this is true, and I am glad. But also we are blamed with other things that go wrong."

"On a hot day like today, tempers are running high, smoldering, ready to ignite." He stroked his gray beard. "Mark, how would you like to carry a letter for me to Paul? He is probably back in Antioch by now."

"You are just looking for a way to get me out of the danger. No, Barnabas, I'll stay with you."

Barnabas thought of other arguments for getting him to leave Cyprus, but he knew they would fail. John Mark had proved that he was no quitter. Barnabas hoped that Paul would discover that fact.

Next day when they went into the city, they learned that the city fathers were preparing an altar in honor of the Emperor. They planned to require every person in Salamis to march by it—a ridiculous scheme calculated to separate the traitors from the loyalists.

Barnabas warned the congregation. He told them it would not be cowardly to flee to another town, reminding them that refugees from Saul's persecution first brought them the good news to Cyprus. They asked what he would do. "I, myself, will someday lose my life. I've known others who died for their faith, and I'm no better than . . ." He thought of Stephen and said, "In fact, not half as good as they."

Barnabas refused to leave Salamis, and John Mark refused to leave his cousin. They spoke to diminished classes. Some of the believers left town and others became afraid to be associated with the church.

Like the warning of the approach of a thunderstorm, the high priest of Zeus insisted on a celebration with proper ceremony. He received full support from the gymnasium people, including Rufus. They set the time for the obeisance, and a local holiday was declared. No one was required to work. The entire population was summoned to the sacrifice for the Emperor.

On that warm day, John Mark and Barnabas remained in the farm house. Nothing eventful happened there. Toward the middle of the afternoon, they saw a figure, half-running and half-stumbling along the road to their place. A young woman had left her watch over the cooled dye-vats of his mother long enough to come with a message. She arrived at their place out of breath but not wanting to rest. She blurted out her message: "They are coming—coming to—arrest you."

"Who?" he asked, knowing the answer.

"The soldiers." She had delivered her breathy message, and she turned to leave.

"Thank you, my friend." He called to her in the road. "Have no fear for yourself." She was running. "Nor for us," he added, doubting that she heard. Barnabas watched her disappear down the road and stood in the doorway, leisurely, as if he had all the time in the world. Suddenly the impact of her message filled his body, as if he had drunk a potion of poison that took time to affect his members. He turned on Mark in a frenzy. "Leave, Mark, leave while there is time."

"If you will come with me."

"No. Two would be in more danger fleeing. I will stay and meet them here. Go back to Jerusalem." He looked at the expressionless face of the man who had deserted Paul almost ten years before and returned to the safety of his mama's lap in Jerusalem. Mark did not look like the same person. His hair was streaked with white just above his ears. Tiny lines were drawn around his eyes. "Please," Barnabas urged.

"I am not afraid to die."

Barnabas knew that John Mark meant it, yet he reasoned, "You are young. You have a great work to do."

"No, my cousin, I am not going to leave you."

The Son of Encouragement knew that his own fear was not personal, but for John Mark and his writings. They must be saved at any price. "At any price," he said aloud, and the writer looked to see what he meant. "I was thinking of the price you would have to pay to save me," said the encourager, who had seldom asked any personal privilege from his kinsman.

"I would pay any price to save your life," said Mark, simply and dry-eyed.

"Here's the price—humbling yourself before Sergius Paulus," said Barnabas. He was not accustomed to asking favors, and he found the words bitter on his tongue. "Not worship, but friendship. You could ask for executive clemency, and he certainly would grant it."

"Even though he gives no sign of believing in Christ?"

"Yes. His memories are not dead. He will remember Paul's miracle. He will do something for us." Barnabas knew if Mark could be removed from the danger for a short time, he might be able eventually to save himself and his manuscripts. Strangely, he recalled the rudeness of his mother when she got Barnabas to leave the dangerous town of Salamis; now he understood her motives. His were similar. Like a father he spoke to Mark, "Hurry. Take your writing with you, and let nothing happen to it. They will be here any moment." Barnabas didn't delay his cousin long enough for a final embrace or a prayer—he wished for both. As he let him out the back door, Barnabas caught his cousin's arm for an added instruction. "Mark, make two copies of everything." He pushed him away and shouted further orders to him as he turned behind a storage building. "Keep them in two separate places. Make sure they are preserved. People will need . . ."

Barnabas heard pounding on the door that was louder than the pounding in his heart. He met four soldiers and identified himself. He invited them to come in from the heat of the day, and not one of them noticed the figure disappearing on the road west.

Barnabas invited them to eat an evening meal with him before returning to the garrison. He was surprised that his offer was accepted. He set plates for the four guards. He dropped a plate that shattered into tiny triangular shivers. When he fell to his knees to pick up the pieces, he prayed. In his mind he said, *Lord, forgive my trembling. Save Mark. Preserve his writing. Let your work prosper. And let your servant be worthy to confess Christ even to the death.*

The last free air he breathed before entering the prison was sultry. He found the tiny cell like an oven. He shared it with a prisoner who had been there long enough to develop a repulsive odor and with a young Jew who also had refused to acknowledge the Emperor's divinity that day. He wondered how many other Christians were kept on other levels of the large prison.

In the tedius days of waiting, both cellmates were moved out, the older one for execution for murder and the younger one for release. The loneliness made the temperature of the cubicle his main concern.

One day a rain changed the heat of the prison to a refreshing coolness. Then the moisture turned cold. A persistent rain fell. Its patient dampness seeped into his absorbent heart. He listened to the thumping, tapping drops splatter on the stones of the window sill. He despised waiting for courts, judges, and official documents. He wondered if an angel might deliver him from prison, as had happened to Peter. He wondered if he might be left for dead, as had happened to Paul at Lystra. If these events were too miraculous to expect, maybe his execution would be delayed until Mark had a chance to see the governor, whose heart might be softened to grant a stay of execution.

He wondered if Mark would find Sergius Paulus at all. It would not matter if the trip to Paphos only saved his cousin's life and scrolls. He recalled his last words to his cousin, "Make two copies of everything."

Barnabas heard the dripping rain outside. It had a melancholy sound. The air in the cell was chilly. He bent his legs under him in order that they would be covered by his threadbare cloak. He had tried to sleep, but the chill had kept him awake. As on other nights, he wondered what would happen the next day.

He decided to amuse himself with an inventory of his life. He smiled. A former wrestler had allowed himself to be taken prisoner by four clumsy little soldiers. A former property owner in the hills of Cyprus was confined to a dismal little cell. The contrasts were almost humorous.

He ran his stubby fingers through the wavy hair, no longer black but now the color of dirty snow. He coughed for such a long time that he wondered if his lungs might cheat the executioner. In the prison he had time to think, but the chill of the cell and the putrid odors from down the hall seemed to anesthetize his brain.

He heard a prisoner on the floor above him whispering a

message to a waiting wife down in the street. Barnabas thought of himself as a dying man who would leave behind no children. He had always wished for children. He had imagined himself many times at the head of a table surrounded by several curly-headed children. He could see a kind woman at the opposite end—with a face like Sarah's —assisting him in the prayers and instructions. He recalled the old saying: "As arrows are in the hand of a mighty man; so are children of the youth. Happy is the man that hath his quiver full of them: they shall not be ashamed, but they shall speak with the enemies in the gate." The verse gave him a new thought: A man's children will speak to the enemies. His own John Mark was then negotiating with the enemy. Surely he was like a son. He was exactly like he would have wanted a son to be. He was not a disappointment like the boy Jacob. He wondered if Jacob might see Paul in Rome; he prayed that he would.

Barnabas thought how many nights he had yearned for a wife to share his bed with him. He had wanted a quiet life of family pleasure, but such had been impossible. He had been driven forward by an urge stronger than reproduction; he had tried to carry God's message to lost people.

If John Mark were like a son to Barnabas, surely Mark's converts would be his spiritual grandchildren. He recited, "Children's children are the crown of old men." He was placing his hope on his own spiritual sons, Mark, Titus, Timothy, Thorn Bush, and the rest. He was placing his hope in them and in their converts. It was a satisfying thought to one whose family name was dying out with him: A more important name, Christian, would continue to live.

He pulled himself up to the window to see if some messenger that morning might be coming from Mark or from Paul or from some unrevealed miracle that God had in store. He mused, *But miracles were never for me—always for Paul.* Now his memories centered around Paul. He recalled how they had made the trips together to Jerusalem, to Cyprus, and back to Jerusalem. It was tragic that such wonderful days had been marred by petty differences. Now he could not even remember the things that had seemed important back then.

He longed for an opportunity to talk with Paul. In his excitement of thinking what he would say, Barnabas began to speak aloud, through the wall and toward the sea: "Paul, you were not wrong for wanting to be careful about the missionary trips. Such an undertaking is far too important to base on flimsy wishes. Yet, I put the same trust in Mark that I put in you. Paul, we were both wrong, and we were both right. You now can see that Mark is trustworthy. But he's not cut out to be an evangelist. He will make a greater contribution to the world through his manuscripts; these are his power and glory."

Barnabas sighed. "Soon the executioner will come. The guards assured me it would happen. Dear brother Paul, I wonder if the same fate doesn't await you. We have been beaten and suffered many other hardships together. I could wish we were together in death as we were for those few wonderful years of life. Yet I am thankful you are not dying—the world needs you. Much more than it needs me. The world desperately needs your life and teachings. Save as much time as possible. Don't seek martyrdom. Leave your thoughts in writing."

The jailer, with two helpers, came to the door. He was a

big man, with large shoulder muscles, but he kept looking at the floor, as if he were embarrassed by this duty.

"You're to be released. The proconsul ordered it."

Barnabas exhaled a sigh. Others, both Jews and believers who had refused to worship a mere man, were loosed from their cells. They walked toward the door, and he felt weak.

At the entrance, all the other released prisoners stopped, but he stumbled out into the humid afternoon. The rain had stopped, and the sun poked long fingers of light through the clouds. His eyes could not adjust to the brilliance, and he had trouble seeing whether anyone was in the street. However, toward the next corner, he sensed a pack of people, mumbling. A woman's shrill voice split the silence: "Whose fault was it?"

Someone pointed to Barnabas. "His fault."

The crowd on the narrow street closed in on him. Dogs barked. The people were all strangers—even though they were from his hometown. He didn't know them by name, but he recognized what they were. In the crowd was a shrill voice that belonged to a skinny woman with protruding eyes like one he had seen at Iconium. In the mob was a Baruch, one who had studied law and tried to defend it with an ever-ready shout of "blasphemy." In the pack was a hawk. There was a familiarity about them. All these people had been a part of a mob he had seen grab a slave in the Temple. They also had taken part in the stoning of Paul at Lystra.

Barnabas loosed a wild glance down an alley to see help coming. A young man with a husky voice yelled, "Stop." He recognized Elymas. The crowd turned him back with their threats, and Barnabas saw nothing except blazing eyes of the haters. He heard the clomping sandals of curious people running to see something exciting.

On that sunlit day, a shadow passed over the paving stones. God blew a refreshing breeze down the alleyway. Barnabas sensed something about to happen, something as thrilling as the restoring of sight to a blind man. The sun felt warm on his hair and beard. With belligerence, he thought, *Don't give me a miracle now, Lord. It wouldn't be in keeping with the rest of my life. It would be inconsistent. It would be wasted power.*

Barnabas mused that it was a wonder he had not run against a wild herd like this one long before. He perceived they were animals, lusting for blood. They felt, without knowing why, compelled to make a kill. He saw them moving in a deliberate ritual of sacrifice.

It was too late for tears, but not for prayers, not for memories. He touched the parchment fragment of the crucifixion, given to him by John Mark, now tied to a cord around his neck. In his heart, he held to the belief that he would see his Messiah that same day.

"Troublemaker!" someone screamed.

Suddenly something sharp flew through the air and struck his forehead with the same impact of that beam from long ago on the Temple bridge. Other stones hit their bloody target. Sprawled in the street, he looked up to see the same man who spat on his mother's door, pursing his lips in satisfaction.

"I forgive you. God have mercy on you."

A strange calm, like the waters of baptism, rolled over him, and he said *"Shalom,* Paul."